What people say abou
The Mastery of Manag

"*The One-Minute Manager* raised our consciousness by convincing us of the importance of praising. *The Mastery of Management* goes one step further by teaching us how to determine and deliver just the right kind of praise to each person."

- JOHN REHFELD
Seiko Instruments USA

"Taibi Kahler has identified why people do what they do. It is must reading for any of us who hope to lead or manage or motivate other people!"

- MAX CLELAND
Former Georgia Senator
Former Chief of the U.S. Veterans Administration

"If communication is the key to success, then miscommunication is costing us a fortune. *The Mastery of Management* is an excellent tool for understanding why we miscommunicate with others and how we can change this unproductive pattern. A must read for every manager."

- STEVE QUIST
VP/General Manager, Measurement Division
Rosemount, Inc.

"In today's competitive and fast moving environment, it seems easy to overlook the value of personal communication. *The Mastery of Management* helps to keep us focused on the personal needs of our team and enables us to deliver the right kind of praise to each person."

- ROBERT S. PARKE
Sanford Corporation

"*The Mastery of Management* is the key that unlocked our communication blind sports. It has unleashed greater effectiveness in our teamwork and execution, and helped our organization rediscover the joys of working together."

- F. T. RENSHAW
President & CEO
Research, Inc.

What people say about Kahler Seminars:

"The Process Communication Model provides a framework for evaluating the information one wishes to communicate and the best means for doing so with various recipients of that information. I appreciate Taibi taking the time to provide the special seminar for us and look forward to many years of making use of what I learned."

— SENATOR HILLARY CLINTON

"We've started changing the way we communicate with people and are getting positive results: clearer problem definitions, less 'turf protecting' during conflicts, clearer expectations, shorter and more productive meetings, more fun at work."

— ED F. JEFFREY
Opryland USA, Inc.

"Process Communication for Managers really got into the 'nuts and bolts' of the system, and developed a very strong communication skills habit that continues to serve us quite well."

— JAMES P. RODDY, III
President
Roddy Coca-Cola Bottling Co.

"The Process Communication Model is, without reservation, the most effective thing I have learned about understanding the behavior of myself and others. PCM enables me to take all of that seemingly unrelated behavior and make it understandable."

— LARRY M. SHORT
General Manger
Northern Operations
TRW Ross Gear Division

"Through the years I have attended many programs and sessions at various conferences offered by Boys & Girls Clubs of America. The presentation on "Critical Communication Skills" proved to be the most meaningful."

-Thomas G. Garth,
National Director of the
Boys & Girls Clubs of America

"Terrific, terrific! I have had the opportunity to participate in many conferences and seminars over the past 28 years in labor education and truly, your Process Communication Seminar is one of the finest I have ever had the opportunity to attend."

-Arthur F. Kane,
Director of Education,
International Brotherhood of Teamsters

"The Process Communications Management Workshop I just attended must rate as a highlight of my business seminar experiences. "

-John E. Renfeld,
Vice President & General Manager, Toshiba

"You have been a tremendous asset to us in building the type of *team* we want to be successful when selling our products to both employers and employees. The sales management team has been extremely pleased and I have noticed a considerable improvement in our understanding of the various personalities we work with both internally and externally."

-Julie Marshall,
Senior Vice President, USAble Life

"The Atlanta Knights can't thank you enough for sharing with us the power of Process Communication Management.

Your PCM training is already making a difference in our advertising sales, not only in helping attract new clients, but in servicing our current clients as well. By better understanding the corporate "decision makers" that we are pursuing and already working with, we feel that the Knights have an advantage over the competition.

Not only has PCM provided the Knights with an effective communication tool to help us reach our sales goals, but the skills we learned in your training have helped produce clearer channels of communication in the office, resulting in a happier and more efficient staff. Your training or detecting early warning signs of distress and avoiding potential conflicts has been invaluable!"

-Mike Sammond,
Director of Fulfillment/Advertising Sales,
Atlanta Knights Professional Hockey

"Process Communication is an understandable and useful tool, and it can be used in all of my interactions. I will be able to use this in teaching clergy. The application of this material for clergy in looking at their parish and how they function is fascinating."

-George Doebler,
UT Medical Center,
Chaplain

"EPSON is a Japanese company and PCM has also helped me to better understand the personality of the organization and my colleagues in Japan. Again the critical communication process has been improved by understanding their needs and interaction styles, incorporating these into the communication system, and recognizing problem areas."

-Trevor J. Lee,
Director, Vertical Markets,
EPSON America, Inc.

"As Principal of a Catholic School in Washington, D.C., I have found Process Communication's staff development program helpful for our teachers to better meet the needs of our "at risk" students. The PCM model enabled our teachers to better understand our students and their needs by identifying the personality types and ways to get those needs met. Once teachers were able to accomplish this in a positive way the students could meet their teacher's expectations. Our teachers have learned how to interpret negative behavior and to acquire new ways to intervene effectively with students. As a result their classrooms have become more productive."

-Mary Jane Jackson,
Principal,
St. Peter's Interparish School

"Process Communication has facilitated relationship building and has made what is a people intensive organization more successful. And as an aside, unquestionably the model has assisted the participants in their own personal lives, which in a direct way impacts their productivity in our organization.

An organization which believes in the development of people can profit immensely from the incorporation of the Process Communication Model. We have, and will continue to recommend it in our client environments where there is an interest in positive and constructive organizational change."

-Malcolm E. Lehman, Ed.D.,
Director, Learning and Development,
Arkansas Blue Cross Blue Shield

We have ample evidence to demonstrate to those interested in improving education to suggest that Process Communication can play in school improvement. In fact, we're so convinced of the value of the program that we would like to invite those who may be interested in using your information to visit our district and talk to our personnel about how they view the program.

-William F. Wright, Ed.D.,
Superintendent of Schools,
Apache Junction, Arizona

"Your workshop truly was peak experience for me. I think that the fine quality of your workshop is a combination of three main factors. Process Communication is a well developed model which allows for simplicity and complexity in understanding human behavior – the role playing and experiential components of the workshop also greatly enhance my learning experience. I have already begun to incorporate PCM into my work as a therapist. I highly recommend the PCM workshop to anyone in the mental health profession and to anyone who wants to learn how to communicate better with people. This workshop is the best workshop I have ever attended."

-Toby Weaver, Ph.D.,
The University of Tennessee

"The three days I spent in your Process Communication seminar was the best time spent by this agency toward improving internal and external communications – in improving, what we do and how we do it. Thanks for presenting your program to our key executives. We are all abuzz with new techniques – you really did charge up the batteries.

-Franklin Bradley,
Chairman & CEO,
Notch/Bradley

"Your seminar was outstanding. Our staff has continued to talk about their new understanding of themselves."

-James B. McGhee, M.D.,
Medical Director, HCA

"We are better individuals, a better team and a better company because of Process Communication. It was one of the most important professional courses I have ever taken because the concepts can be used everyday and benefit all parties of the interaction."

–JOE B. HOUCHIN
President & CEO
Proton Pacific, Inc.
Real Estate Investments

"Process Communication was not just another boring management training. It greatly exceeded my expectations and has turned out to be the most valuable skills development course I have ever taken."

–KENNETH WENDEL
Director of Quality
Unisys Corporation

"The impact of the Process Communication seminar on my personal health has been profound."

–ELIZABETH MCMULLEN
Tennessee Valley Authority

"Process Communication has ample detail without being over-whelming. It is very clear and presented without the jargon which often obscures the message. The Kahler Personality Inventory is the most revealing instrument I have ever used to understand myself and others. I have been richly rewarded by the experience of the seminar both personally and professionally."

–MARY ESBENSHADE
Whittle Communications

"Process Communication Management is a three day training course which every lawyer should take. Not only does PCM make it possible for lawyers to determine the best and most efficient way of communicating with their clients, it permits trial lawyers a coherent and intelligible guide for selecting members of a jury and for determining the best means of portraying a case before those jurors. I would strongly recommend that every member of the bar participate in this program."

–CHARLES FELS
Attorney-at-Law

"The Kahler Experiencing Excellence seminar is the best I have ever had to help me manage. It had concrete ideas for dealing with people. I think it should be mandatory and would be extremely useful for principals and vice-principals."

–JOANNE DRAPER
East York Collegiate Institute

"Process Communication Management is a valuable tool that I use in the training and supervision of staff whose performance is critical to an abused child's life. Abused children cannot afford the risk of miscommunication."

–SHARON PALLONE
Executive Director
SCAN America, Inc.

The Mastery of Management

or, How To Solve The Mystery of Mismanagement

Taibi Kahler Ph.D.

Distributed by:

Kahler Communications, Inc.
11815 Hinson Rd.
Little Rock, Arkansas 72212
(501) 372-3765
kahlercom@aristotle.net

ISBN 0-9701185-2-X

Printed in the United States of America.

Price: $14.95 (U.S.)

dedicated
to the memory of
Dr. Hedges Capers

Forward

Having experienced working with high performing executives for years, I am convinced that those who possess both superior leadership and superior management skills have in common superior people skills. They are not limited to working well with a select few, but rather have the innate or learned ability to communicate with a wide variety of people in clear and even inspiring ways.

These exceptional motivators of others have discovered a universal truth of communication: *how we say something is even more important than what we say*. While the message itself is important, it is secondary to the process by which it is consistently delivered. It is truly the process that becomes the message, not merely the content of the words. While this has been long recognized, we have only recently understood how this took place. Dr. Taibi Kahler's lasting contribution to our society will be this well-researched, systematic model of the anatomy of successful interpersonal communication. *The Mastery of Management* is the mastery of undestanding how to use what we are taught in business schools. It is the answer to the question: after the MBA, now what?

More than 800,000 people in North America have experienced the Kahler Process Model since its conception. Universally applicable across cultures, his accompanying validated profiles and seminar materials have been translated and implemented in twelve other countries. Dr. Kahler's Six Personality Types were identified statistically, then correlated with individual:

- character strengths
- management styles
- personality parts
- channels of communication
  (the way people prefer to talk to one another)
- environmental preferences
- psychological motivators
- perceptions
  (the way people experience the world)
- degrees of distress
  (predictable ways someone sabotages his or her personal and professional life through sequences of miscommunication and mismanagement)

Instead of a dry, textbook approach giving endless definitions and statistical correlations, Dr. Kahler has written this book with simplicity and application in mind. His sound theories are presented in a refreshingly straight forward and commonsense manner. He invites the reader into experiencing the personal and professional world of each of the six Personality Types, and then gives a daily, weekly, and monthly action plan of how best to communicate and manage each.

In my twenty plus years of consulting with senior executives in Fortune 500 companies, I have not found a more universally useful model than is explained in this important body of knowledge. It is written in such a subtly simple way that I caution even the sophisticated manager to study his work literally line by line to understand and appreciate Dr. Kahler's discovery of the very building blocks of successful communication and management.

This is a gift worth savoring.

-Brad Spencer, Ph.D.

Prologue

Need we step into the thickening fog of an uncertain midnight, then hail a hansom cab on some lonely cobblestone lane to experience the adventures of a good mystery?

Ha! Certainly not, my winsome adventurer. A rather fine mystery can be yours in the sphere of your own influence. It is the classic mystery of human behavior. Why do other people do what they do....and what, pray tell, will they do next? Deduce the solution, and a new realm of success and leadership will be your ample reward.

For now, however, let us look closely at the facts of the case before us without further delay. The facts are these:

Six career-oriented managers of a major American corporation are about to rouse from their slumber to face another day. Three are women, three are men: each is capable, responsible, and successful. Life at home and work moves forward on an even keel. The commonplace rules. Prospects of radical change are faint and distant. As yet another halcyon day dawns, an underlying element of mystery floats in the backwaters of each character's mind. Late yesterday the CEO's secretary had telephoned to schedule a senior staff conference for 2 p.m. today. A reason for the meeting was not tendered, only the admonition: under no circumstances should you miss it. Quiet inquiries and oblique queries from the more curious of our characters had ended at the same stone wall of silence and secrecy.

Upon that meeting the whole mystery of this tale of action and reaction will turn. It is a small puzzle in the morning, but what complex conundrum shall it be in the evening? Could six highly successful professionals change in the course of one day from a posture of absolute security to one of abject confusion and deepening despair?

We shall see, we shall see. The key questions are these: what truths about character and personality will become evident to you through your observations of another's actions, speech, demeanor, appearance, and environment? What link could there be between mismanagement behaviors and psychological need? And how can your powers of deduction and reasoning unravel mysteries of human behavior?

As you read this tale, we ask that you view mismanagement as a crime. We urge you to search not only for the methods of the crime, but also for the motives behind the crime. We will present ample evidence to assist you in deducing a solution to this pervasive form of criminal behavior, which victimizes American business and industry with low productivity, low morale, shoddy worksmanship, and downright sabatoge. And we will show you how to put the solution into action, to interject the mastery of management into your daily affairs by restoring productivity and the spirit of success to a daily business scene gone awry.

Mismanagement is a mystery only as long as people and behavior are a mystery. You can clear up the mystery by understanding the dynamic nature of a person's Personality Type as well as the attendant psychological needs that motivate each person to be successful, to accomplish, and to achieve.

A few of us have already looked into the matter. Indeed, you may perceive that we have learned a great deal. The problems of human behavior present features of very exceptional interest. And the mastery of management requires that you sharpen your wits, open your eyes, and extend your reach to encompass the attitude and manner of those who share your realm of being.

One last note before we plunge into the drama. Each of the six major characters represents a pure, exaggerated Personality Type, and each is stereotyped by gender. We have designated Reactor, Rebel, and Dreamer as feminine characters, Workaholic, Persister, and Promoter as masculine characters. In the world of flesh and bones, however, Ruby Reactor could just as well be Roger Reactor, and Walter Workaholic could be Wanda Workaholic. Most of the facts and conclusions about these six pure types are relative to both sexes.

But let's put aside this digression into exaggerated types and sexual stereotypes to consider a most pertinent link in the chain of masterly reasoning: The character strengths, management styles, environmental preferences, and perceptions of our six characters are universal. They symbolize facets of personality you will face every day in the world of business. We ask you to polish your understanding of these elemental sides of human nature with care. By learning to identify the subtle aspects of behavior and the shifting phases of personality with skill and attention, you will profoundly enhance your ability to lead and inspire others.

My dear reader, **I challenge you to** surpass yourself. I invite you to sharpen your management, communication, and motivational skills while you solve the mysteries of personality and discover the secret to the mastery of management in your profession.

Taibi Kahler, Ph.D.

Contents

The Characters
Beginning on Page 13

The Scene
Beginning on Page 39

The Plot
Beginning on Page 65

The Crime
Beginning on Page 79

The Solution
Beginning on Page 97

Epilogue
Beginning on Page 145

A Postscript
Beginning on Page 157

The Characters

The Characters

A
great detective
of Victorian London
once remarked,
"Human nature is a
strange mixture."
Quite so! There is
something in everyone's
character that surely will
fascinate you if you direct
the art of reasoning toward
the careful scrutiny of
human nature, especially
personality. Therefore,
let us gently lift the roofs
of six houses and peep in
at the rousings of our
characters on this cold
and wet Tuesday
morning. Let us
peruse their actions
and, by Jove, even
listen to their
thoughts. It is our duty
to see what inferences
may be drawn about
this case, which
promises to be an
absolutely
unique one.
It begins!

The Characters

- **R**uby **R**eactor
- **P**aul **P**ersister
- **W**alter **W**orkaholic
- **D**oris **D**reamer
- **R**ita **R**ebel
- **P**eter **P**romoter

Walter Workaholic,

rousing from his slumber, hears the disk jockey blaring from the alarm clock radio: "Good morning, everybody! It's another wet day with a 30 per cent chance of snow in the city." Walter grumbles as he pulls the covers over his head. *"Do they mean 30 per cent between the hours of 7 a.m. and 12 noon, or 7 a.m. Tuesday to 7 a.m. Wednesday? What time is it, anyway? Can I sleep a few more minutes? What was it I was dreaming? I can't recall. Maybe somebody will invent a machine that detects when a person's dreaming and then awakens him and records his recollections while he can still remember his dream. Interesting idea, Walt! But what's the market value?"* Walter rolls over, looks at the time. *"Is it my day to drop the kids off? No. Geeze, Joyce is already up."*

The path to Walter's bathroom passes through the kids' room. He accidently kicks a toy. *"Toys on the floor again. How many times do I have to tell the sitter, 'Will you have them put their toys away. It teaches them responsibility.' I could break my neck in the middle of the night with that fire-truck, hook-and-ladder trap."*

Walter smells the aroma of coffee drifting from the kitchen. "Thank goodness for Mr. Coffee. A time and life saver." He takes a seat in the bathroom and simultaneously shaves with an electric razor. The clean, functional, orderly character of the room begins to impart a sense of bearing to the morning. *"The big one today. Two o'clock and something's up. I wonder....maybe a merger, but why? A major project to begin? A reorganization? We'll see."*

Brushing his teeth with generic toothpaste, Walter thinks about baths and showers, orderliness and thoroughness. *"I can't understand why people won't shower off after their baths. You just don't get clean without a final rinse. It's like going to college, taking nothing but electives, attending all the social functions, and then thinking you have an education. If you take a shower, the rinsing water is the only way to really get clean. In college, a person must apply himself and take the required courses if he wants to achieve knowledge."* Walter takes a few seconds to study the color of his gums. *"Who would brush their teeth after their shower? It's illogical to stand there cold and wet while you're brushing."*

His ritual of preparation may be predictable, but it's also highly efficient. In the shower, Walter weighs last night's argument at the dinner party: *"Joyce still doesn't get it. Said I was 'justifying' when I argued with Randy about the value of neatness and order in daily affairs. One course in psychology and I'm 'justifying.' Why wasn't I 'rationalizing?' Fact is, I was just being logical."*

Walter **pays particular attention to** his choice of clothing because of the special afternoon meeting. *"I certainly want to dress appropriately. Anything neat and clean."* He sniffs a suit jacket. *"If the kids let the dog or cat in again, it's to the city pound. I find it more than coincidental that an anagram of pets is pest."* Anticipation of the day's coming event sends his mind racing further. *"I spent a lot of time designing these shelves so I can have my socks in the right places -- all color matched. The cleaning lady is doing a fine job. My shoes are all in the right place. So are the shirts. Good. With the hangers all pointing the same way, and two inches apart. It's enough trouble getting laundered shirts home and still unwrinkled, let alone wrinkling them by pushing them all together on that closet rod."*

On his way to the kitchen for juice and toast, Walter looks through a window just in time to see the paper boy passing by. *"Great, just great. A rainy day and this kid throws the paper onto a wet porch. The paper, I might add, that is noticeably bereft of protective plastic. Smart. He's got a lesson to learn about supply and demand and customer satisfaction."*

Walter decides to read the paper on the way to work. *"I can always count on twenty minutes delay at the 40th and Main traffic jam."* He gives Joyce a peck on the cheek, asks her if supper will be ready at 6 o'clock, and strides briskly to the garage.

The route to the office is typically congested. As traffic slows to a crawl, Walter surveys the interior of his car. *"Still a dependable machine. Nothing fancy, but American built. Twenty-eight miles to the gallon and consistently performs to specs. A darn good buy!"* He turns his attention again to the day ahead: *"Newspaper's still damp. Might as well run down my agenda while the traffic clears. Let's see, when I get to the office...."*

Ruby Reactor

slips quietly from her comfortable little niche under the soft sheets of her bed and pauses to feel the warm pile carpet beneath her feet. *"Feels gooood,"* she reflects. *"I just love to squiggle my toes in the smooth strands."* Alive and happy and filled with a sense of harmony, she stretches her arms high above her head and prepares to ease into another day.

Outside, a soft rain falls. She enjoys the pitter patter on the roof. *"Oh, what a cozy, rainy day,"* Ruby reflects. *"Just love it."* She looks at the soundly sleeping man on the other side of their bed. *"Bob works so hard for us. I'll be quiet so he can sleep a little longer. He's been so caring lately. I love him when he's like that."*

Ruby's bathroom is a bright and cheerful place of sweet smells, fluffy towels, and lush plants. She opens a cabinet filled to overflowing with cosmetics. *"Oh, no -- another wrinkle,"* she observes. *"Am I really 30 now? That sounded old when I was 20. Do I look 30?"* She turns away from the mirror and sips her cup of freshly brewed coffee -- *"the aroma is delicious"* -- then turns again to the image in the mirror. *"Honey, just put on your make-up and you'll be fine. I want to look pretty and successful at the two o'clock meeting with the senior vice president today. He said he has some important news for all of us. I feel like dressing in fall colors today. And I really like this new lip gloss. I hope Bob does."*

Ruby **likes to put on her make-up** before fetching the newspaper from the porch. *"You just never know who you might see, and besides, it's a good way to get in touch with the day,"* she muses. There's the paper boy now, running late because of the rain. "Thank you, Tommy," she says. "Want to borrow an umbrella? I don't want you to catch a cold." The paper is wet. *"I'll read this later after it drys out. I wish it had a 'Parade' section like on Sundays. Oh, well, I've got my new 'People' magazine."* Bob shuffles into the kitchen. Ruby greets him warmly, then excuses herself to begin dressing -- an intricate, creative process. They make small talk during her short breaks from her dressing table. *"I just know he likes me in this color. It really does match my mood today,"* she decides after carefully studying her image in the mirror. *"I'll buy him some of his favorite cologne today -- just a little 'I love you' gift."*

After thirty minutes of careful dressing and primping, Ruby is hugging her man good-bye and telling him how handsome he looks in his new sportscoat. On the way out the door, she snags her hose. A moment of panic races across her mind. *"I wish I could just call in sick when this happens."* On second glance, the snag is barely noticeable. Ruby grabs an extra pair of hose, hugs Bob again, and dashes into the rainy day.

Ruby's car, like many of her possessions, brought very special memories to mind. She and Bob picked it out together, *"and he was helpful. He just doesn't have my eye for style and color. I still love my car. My own, first car, and it still smells almost brand new. I'm so glad it came with this interior. The colors match, and it's very comfortable."*

On the freeway, traffic begins to back-up, then slows to a crawl. Ruby quickly surveys the traffic jam before taking a longer look at her reflection in the vanity mirror. *"Is this the right shade of red for me? Not too brassy, I hope. I'd die if people at the office thought I looked brassy."* She smiles. *"Classy yes! But brassy -- God forbid!"*

The honking of a hundred horns from others caught in the same traffic jam clamors in the morning dampness, but Ruby is oblivious to it all. Her feelings of peacefulness are too great for any earthly dissonance. She visualizes Bob. *"He wants to wait another year, I know, but I want a little girl. I'd love a boy, but a little girl....I'd make dresses for her, fix her room with frills and ruffles and...."*

Suddenly the jam breaks. Traffic roars ahead. *"Family.... Now, Ruby, you do have another family! And you're going to see them this very Tuesday morning at work."*

Paul Persister

awakes, alert and rested. As he reaches to turn off the radio alarm, he hears the announcer report, "Hi, and a good Tuesday morning to you. It's a rainy 30 degrees...." Paul quickly looks outside. *"I don't believe it's that cold. I'll check my own thermometer. Besides, if it were 30 degrees it would be sleeting or snowing."* "Wake up, Kathleen," he says, slipping into a pair of warm slippers. "I believe we've got a wet one ahead of us."

In the expansive master bathroom, Paul turns on his built-in Sony TV. Commentators are discussing yesterday's presidential news conference. *"I really admire his courage, especially with such an emotive issue,"* Paul reasons as he turns off the stylized Kohler faucet. *"Who was it that said, 'The best lack all conviction?' I can't buy that."*

Paul slips into his favorite purple robe and walks through his tastefully appointed house to retrieve the newspaper from the front porch. *"I've always admired that Louis XIV look of elegance,"* he considers as he passes the antique writing table in the parlor. *"And the set of Oriental prints on the adjoining wall provides such a pleasing contrast. It'll be nice getting back to Hong Kong this summer to purchase more."*

A **plastic cover has kept the neatly** folded newspaper dry. *"That kind of attention to detail and quality of service is rare in a young person. That paperboy is certainly wise to anticipate. An ounce of prevention, I always say...."*

In the breakfast nook, Kathleen has set warm croissants and imported English Marmalade next to a white porcelain cup of fresh-ground Colombian coffee. "I hope these are as tasty as those fresh deli bagels you served yesterday," he says, taking a seat in the hard-backed, hand-carved chair. "Well, darling, I hope...." she begins, but Paul quickly cuts her off. "I believe the last time we had croissants they were a bit stale. If only the bakery could be more consistent, especially at their prices."

He turns immediately to the business section of the paper. *"I'm going to get home delivery of the Wall Street Journal. Never enough depth in these local reports. Hummm....Consolidated Time-Shares up three points. And I told Walt just last week it was sure to rise."* "This coffee's bitter," he says, glancing at Kathleen. "You sure look tired today. By the way, what do you think about those religious fanatics in the news this morning?"

Before she can respond, Paul answers his own question, then launches another monologue about the day's news. *"She never seems to have an opinion about any-thing....and that coffee....well, she does try....just wish she could do better."* Paul notices a frown on his wife's brow. "Forgive me, darling," he says. "I do value your opinions, you know that. Excuse me, will you? I have to get dressed. Important meeting today."

Standing at the mirror beside his dresser, Paul notices the deep furrows between his eyes. *"I wonder how Mark will weather age?"* he ponders, thinking of his son at the university. *"Or, if he'll ever grow up at all. Lately he's been a complete mystery to me. Will he ever understand the value of responsible behavior and sound judgment? He's wearing such wild clothes lately...."*

Paul adjusts his maroon, striped tie. Double-Windsor knot, of course. He has selected a gray, three-piece suit and black wing-tipped shoes. *"How can one believe in a company represented by someone wearing less than quality attire? No matter what this meeting is about, they know I'm loyal to the core, on board for the duration."*

"**H**ave a nice day, Kathleen," Paul says as he steps outside toward his gray BMW. "Let's plan on eating out tonight." The heavy car door shuts with a sound of precision and authority. *"I find it hard to understand why anybody would acquire an automobile without true investment value. Not me, that's for sure. And one that's safe, too. This hand-crafted beauty will last for a decade and still retain value."*

In the traffic jam, Paul turns up the volume on his custom designed stereo sound system and warily eyes the other vehicles. *"Ah, Vivaldi. How wonderful. But why won't the mayor do something about these incessant traffic jams. Here I am at a complete halt. Hope nobody hits me. Should have brought my memogenda. My priorities today are...."*

Doris Dreamer

hears the alarm buzzer signal the beginning of another day: 6:30 a.m. *"Time to get up."* She looks out the bedroom window. *"Rainy day. Cold and wet. I'll need a warm sweater."*

Doris slips quietly out of bed. The floor is cold, hard. She looks back at the bed and thinks of her solitary domestic lifestyle. *"No one to tell me they want me to do something special for them today."* She shrugs. *"And nobody to crowd this delicious privacy. Guess I'll read for a while."*

A limp, white towel hangs on an otherwise empty rack in her bathroom, a straightforward space void of any frills or pretense. She steps into the shower. *"I really do love my friends. They're really thoughtful. But my time alone in the morning....Don't know what I'd do if I had to share these quiet dawns of mine."*

Oblivious to the cold, damp morning, Doris towels off and puts on a plain cotton bathrobe. She decides to let her long, straight hair dry naturally this morning. *"Hamilton. Edith Hamilton. Wasn't that the author's name? Need to check at the bookstore on the way home today."*

In the kitchen, Doris puts on the kettle and tosses a bran muffin in the toaster oven. Her cat, purring softly, rubs gently against her leg. *"The misty morning. Dark stallion riding out of the mist....What time did they say we have that special meeting at the office? Hope it doesn't last too awfully long...."* The whistling kettle breaks Doris' reverie. She pours boiling water over a Raspberry Delight tea bag. *"I'll get the newspaper while it steeps."*

Damp, bracing air sends a shiver down her spine when she opens the front door to pick up the newspaper. *"San Francisco. Fisherman's Wharf. Maybe I'll find a good recipe in the food section. But that's in Thursday's paper, isn't it?"* On her way back to the kitchen, Doris pauses in front of the bookshelf. She sets the newspaper down on an end table, forgets it, picks out a book about stained glass windows, and shuffles back to the kitchen. She nibbles on the muffin, sips her tea, and browses through the pages of her book in peaceful solitude with the sound of a softly falling winter rain as the only accompaniment.

"Time to to dress," she decides, but not before she fills kitty's bowl with crunchy, dry food. *"And don't forget my vitamins,*

she reminds herself halfway to the bedroom closet. Back in the kitchen, Doris
pours a glass of cold orange juice and
opens a cabinet door. *"Let's see: A, D, C, and
E. Now I can get dressed."*

Doris has to move last night's need-
lepoint off the chair at her dressing table
before she can sit down. *"The fawn. Bambi and
Thumper. Aunt Grayce always liked nature stories. I
think I'll give this one to her next Christmas."* Doris
drags a comb through her hair, reflects on
her image in the mirror: a calm expression, smooth and placid features. *"Forty-one
and hardly a wrinkle. Mother likes that."*

Doris dabs on a minimum of make-up:
just a touch of powder to take the shine
off, a little dab of clear lipstick to keep
from chapping. She's always preferred the
unadorned look. *"Too much of a bother. What
was that Dylan line....Just another painted face on Des-
olation Row."*

The woman who emerges from this
rustic, uncomplicated home to face
another day in the workaday world is
dressed for rain and cold, rather than for

style and fashion. The car she enters is just a vehicle, nothing special in her mind's eye, a utilitarian means of transportation. *"Glad it started right up."* A stray thought turns her mind to music. *"Singing in the rain. Just singing in the rain."* She reaches for the radio, suddenly remembers it has been broken since last week. *"Doesn't matter. Too intrusive sometimes, anyway."*

In the traffic jam on the freeway, Doris takes her place in the long, metallic line with calm resignation. She considers the colors of the other cars, reflects on what a close friend might be doing at this moment, allows her mind to wander as the traffic inches forward. *"That meeting this afternoon. Wonder what's up. Maybe Peter can tell me what to expect. Sure hope it doesn't take too long...."*

Rita Rebel

had heard the bedside radio blasting out the usual wake-up calls: a loud buzzer, and even louder rock 'n roll. But she had buried her head under a pillow and moaned something like, "Go away, turn yourself off," before hitting the snooze control for the second or third time that morning. Now Jordan, her teenaged son and good pal, is shaking Rita's shoulders and imploring: "Get up, mom. You're going to be late for work again."

"Allright, geeze, I'm getting up," she protests. "I can't help it if my alarm clock doesn't work." Rita pulls herself with great reluctance from the familiar territory of bright yellow bed sheets. A ray of humor shines briefly from her half-opened eyes as she grabs a stray sock and tosses it playfully at Jordan. Then she notices the scene outside. "That's great," she mutters with a downward inflection. "A rainy day."

Rita's bathroom is like the other rooms in her "playhouse": colorful, messy, and infused with a spirit of fun. She reaches for the Mickey Mouse soap dish, but only a sliver of soap remains. *"Think I'll wait and look in the mirror after coffee!....I know that electric tooth-brush is around here somewhere,"* but Rita can't find it, so she squeezes a glob of toothpaste into her mouth and brushes with her finger. *"Is morning just a cruel joke some insomniac in power played on the rest of us?"* she groans. *"I....don't....like....it!"*

Jordan bursts in, gulps down a can of Classic Coke, says, "I'm history, see ya later." "Just a minute fast boy," Rita shouts. "How 'bout a big hug for the road?" "Sure, mom, just don't kiss me, you got toothpaste all over your mouth" -- which is just what she does, laughing playfully as she kisses him on his cheek. Jordan is wiping toothpaste off his face on the way out the door, and he's long gone before Rita wonders: *"Look at the time -- he's always making me late. At least I don't have to clean up after his father anymore."*

Reflected in the mirror is a pretty face dominated by lively, friendly eyes. Smile lines encircle those happy eyes, while laugh lines paint corners of time around Rita's mouth. The afternoon at the office crosses her mind. *"Boy, it will really make me mad if they try to institute some 8-to-5, clock punching management philosophy. They've been letting me do my thing lately and I'm having a ball, doing the best work I've ever done."* Never one to linger in self-reflection, Rita grabs a brush and begins to transform her disheveled, unruly hair into something stylish and beautiful.

"C*an't wear that one....too many conservatives at the office,"* she concludes, dismissing her first choice: a daring, multicolored affair, which hangs amid an array of other bright dresses over a pile of shoes and other assorted accessories in her helter-skelter closet. *"At least they can't tell me what underpants to wear."* Rita puts on bright yellow undies with little red lips all over, but her choice of outer garments reflects her worldly wisdom: smartly stylish, yet tasteful and just conservative enough to avoid the judging eye of certain peevish managers.

Rita sings with flair while she dresses, sings along with the high energy rock music playing loudly on her mega-decibel stereo sound system -- the most prominent furnishing in her apartment. It is a trendy, split-level unit in midtown, *"where the streets aren't rolled up and put to bed at midnight."* Rita drags the brush through her hair one last time, searches frantically to locate her purse, grabs a cold piece of last night's pizza, and runs out the door.

She picks up the soggy newspaper to cover her hair, leaps over rain puddles, and flings herself into an old, inexpensive sports car with a leaky roof, a worn carpet -- but, of course, a great sound system. She turns on the radio before trying to start the car. *"Come on, baby. Don't fail me now,"* she urges the engine, which groans sluggishly, then starts with a roar and a puff of smoke. "Allright! Let's get on down the road," Rita shouts with a characteristic laugh. She races to the freeway, but runs smack-dab into a major traffic jam. *"Here I go, rushing around like the March hare to get ready for work, and these tortoises clog up the highway."* Rita fumbles through the newspaper to her favorite section, the cartoon pages. And the office? It's a million miles away.

Peter Promoter

hears the alarm, awakes in an instant. "Let's hit it," he says out loud. He pulls a bedroom curtain aside, notes the rain. *"Doesn't matter. Can't let something like weather slow me down."* Peter activates his audio-cassette player, breathes deeply as the theme to "Rocky" begins to play. With gusto he plunges into his 12-minute Air Force calisthenics routine on the plush, red carpet of the bedroom.

Peter turns the gold-plated faucet handles to hot. In the steamy, invigorating shower stall, he shaves while recalling the excitement of last night. *"Whew, Pete, old boy. A few more like that and you'll get the Don Juan Memorial Award. What a knockout she was!"* He grabs a thick, black towel with "PP" embroidered in gold, dries off quickly, drops the towel to the floor. To Peter's perception, the red and black wallpaper with its satiny texture imparts a feeling of richness and power to the room. The dozen bottles of cologne offer a dynamic freedom of choice. And the empty toilet paper dispenser -- well, that's a momentary inconvenience.

Wasting time in his rented condominium is not one of Peter's favorite pastimes, but he hasn't slipped into full gear just yet. That comes after he spends a moment or two in front of the full-length mirror, flexing his muscles and admiring his physique. *"Let's get it together for the big one today,"* he says to self. *"I'm going to go in loaded for bear and expect fireworks from the boss,"* Peter decides as he considers the mysterious afternoon meeting. *"He can count on me to run with whatever he dishes out."*

In high gear now, Peter chooses his clothes with speed and assurance: a hand-sewn white shirt with monogram and 18-karat gold cuff links, a classy red silk tie, superbly tailored Bill Blass slacks and matching sportscoat, sleek snakeskin belt, and Bally shoes. A diamond nugget ring and thick Italian herringbone gold chain contribute to Peter's bold, dashing demeanor. *"It would take a gemologist to know that these aren't the real thing,"* he chuckles while looking at the impressive diamond ring.

Dressed to kill, Peter strides to his kitchen bar and quickly creates a morning health shake to wash down his daily dose of vitamins. In the hallway, he glances in a mirror, notes how nicely his ruddy complexion matches the red tie, picks out an umbrella with a silver-tipped handle, and moves confidently into the world outside.

Just outside, **Peter crosses paths** with his landlady. She pauses under the canopy to ask for the rent. "Hon, you know me, I'll have it by tonight," he says with a charming lilt and bright smile. "And I'll bring you a special little something for your patience."

In the parking lot he bumps into Herb, one of his neighbors, who is just coming off the night shift with a morning newspaper in hand. "Hey, Herb old buddy, how's it going this bright and rainy morning?" Without waiting for a reply, Peter says, "Listen, you're going to rack right now, we're both getting wet, how's about slipping me the paper? I'll have it back before you're awake. No skin off your nose, right? And listen, I'll put down a bet on the double if you want me to."

Peter **maneuvers the dark green** Jaguar into traffic. *"Don't know if I ever would buy these wheels, but this lease action is OK."* The pace of traffic slows to a standstill. Peter turns to the sports pages. "Should have put a dime on Denver," he grouses.

Peter slips in a motivational tape, searches for a break in the traffic jam. A motorcycle cop passes on the shoulder. Peter pulls out in a blaze of speed and follows until he can exit the expressway.

Echoing the speaker on the tape, Peter tap-tap-taps on the steering wheel and says, "Life is *indeed* nothing more than a chain of opportunities." He looks in his rearview mirror at the long lines of traffic and smiles. "See you later, boys!"

The
Scene

The Scene

Our peep
into the private places of the
mind and heart has shown us some
very interesting things about our
characters, who represent six universal
Personality Types:
Workaholic, Reactor, Persister,
Dreamer, Rebel, and Promoter.
Now let us visit the scene of the
drama, which is the headquarters
complex of a major corporation.
Examine the details of this crime
scene in search of all that is to be
seen, but keep in mind three
areas of special importance.
Look first for *Character Strengths*
because they will provide clues
to Personality Type. Then,
observe how the characters
interact with others. That
will help you identify
Management Styles.
Finally, see if you
can deduce a
Motivational Strategy
for each character
by watching how
they motivate
others.

- **C**haracter **S**trengths

- **M**anagement **S**tyles

- **M**otivational **S**trategy

Walter Workaholic

methodically computes his first hour's schedule and workload even as he strolls briskly through the office complex doors.

"Good morning," Walter says to the security guard. "Will you let me into the computer center, please?" *"Old George really looks tired this morning. I think I'd better say something to perk up his morale."* "Thanks, George," Walter says as George unlocks the door. "You are a man we can count on day in and day out."

Walter glances at his watch. *"Just eight minutes before I have to be at my desk. But I've got to make certain the night staff has the proposal properly collated."* The proposal is Walter's latest extra project, an efficiency study designed to enhance shipping and receiving operations. *"I'm certain this cost effective plan will impress the senior vice president,"* he thinks as he peruses the paperwork. *"After all, it is part of my job description to streamline operations, and I did do it on my own time."* The paperwork is in order. "Good work," he tells the clerk. "Will you make three copies and route them to my office as soon as possible?"

Ruby Reactor,

perfectly attuned to the new day, glides through the front doors of the company office complex as if she were walking on a carpet of air. She feels youthful, useful, and accepted.

"Good morning, George," Ruby says to the security guard, a kindly man with whom she feels a natural affinity. "I heard about your wife being sick. I really feel for both of you. You know how much I care for you and Mary. I've made some of my special chicken soup for her. If you don't mind, I'd like to bring it by tonight."

Ruby gives George a warm hug, then joins the brisk flow of human traffic. In the hallway she sees Cindy, a young copy writer on her public relations staff. "Hello, young lady," Ruby says, putting an arm around Cindy's shoulders as she walks alongside her. "I want you to know I understand how difficult a time you've been having. How about sitting down with me for a minute so I can share a solution."

Paul Persister

is pondering the afternoon meeting as he arrives at the office complex a half hour early. *"I believe upper management will continue to recognize my commitment to the organization,"* he decides. *"And it's excellent timing that I've just volunteered to serve on the selection committee for the new training program. They'll realize that my committee work involves extra time I'm not paid for. I've just got to be sure the boss knows the full extent of my contributions."*

Paul notices that the young man who was hired just last week as a company courier is leaving the building with a bank satchel in one hand and a deposit slip in the other. *"How many potential robbers are seeing the same thing I'm seeing?"* Paul asks himself as the young runner dashes outside. *"I need to make a memo for that young man's supervisor suggesting that all couriers put company money in a nondescript valise to attract less attention and cut down on risk to company funds. I'll do it as soon as I get to my desk."*

On the way to his office, Paul stops by the audio-visual room to confirm his reservation of a slide projector and screen for Wednesday's talk to the Downtown Kiwanis Club Luncheon.

Doris Dreamer

sits quietly in her car in the parking lot, transfixed for a moment by a sudden idea about the office complex environment, a novel idea triggered by a recent article in "Popular Science." *"It may solve the recurrent problem of drastic changes in conference room temperatures,"* she muses. Imaginative solutions to mundane problems seem to spring naturally from Doris' introspective mind.

The morning rain enhances Doris' reflective nature. She makes a quick note of the new idea for room temperature control, then pauses again to watch the frantic action in the parking lot. People are dashing to and fro in vain attempts to keep dry. Their umbrellas and head coverings are as diverse as the sea of personality flowing through humanity. *"Interesting image,"* she observes. *"Amusing....to a degree."* In marked contrast to the rainy day action, Doris opens her umbrella and walks calmly into the office complex. She slips quietly past the crowded break room and makes a straight path toward her office.

Rita Rebel

stands in the middle of a loud and laughing group of coworkers in the office break room. She shows off a new electronic version of Rubik's cube. "OK, Rita, but let's hope you don't solve this cube the way you solved the first one," an office buddy was saying. "At least not before we get a shot or two at solving it ourselves." Like the ancient emperor who had unsheathed his sword to cut the Gordian knot, Rita had gained a degree of office fame by once breaking a Rubik's cube into its many parts to help her solve its mysteries.

"Hey, where's it at, D.D.," Rita shouts out the door to Doris, whose only acknowledgement is a simple nod. "And you, John, where'd you get that wild cowboy hat?" she says to the new staff artist as he walks, dripping raindrops, into the room. "Are you doing Redford or Newman?" In a twinkling, John quips: "You can call me Raindance." His lightening wit, knowledge of movie trivia, and spontaneous humor elate Rita. "Raindance -- that's fast on the draw, artist! We'll do fine."

Peter Promoter

had taken the long way 'round to the company offices so he could window shop in the retail concourse located on the opposite side of the office complex entrance. The concourse was extra crowded because of the rain. Peter liked the hustle and bustle. It added a touch of excitement to the brisk morning.

To Peter's surprise, he noticed that the elegant woman approaching one of the escalators was the senior vice president's talkative wife. *"It's not the action to just walk up to her and make conversation,"* Peter reckoned ....when he suddenly saw that her mink coat was about to be snared by the escalator's steps. *"How opportune!"* He dashed to her side to prevent the unfortunate accident. "Oh, goodness, thanks, Peter," she said. "My privilege, Mrs. Watson," he replied. "Don't let that gorgeous fur get even one blemish on it. Especially a mink that looks so stunning on its wearer. By the way, heard anything about that important meeting your husband has scheduled for this afternoon?"

Character strengths....

are a major source of personal and professional success. Observing someone's behavior over a period of time allows us to determine their major character strengths.

Using the character studies you have just read (and observed through your mind's eye), match the behavioral responses on the next page to test your new knowledge. Which three clusters of strengths (traits) fit each Personality Type?

Personality Type

1. Reactor.
2. Workaholic.
3. Persister.
4. Dreamer.
5. Rebel.
6. Promoter.

Character Strengths

A. Spontaneous, Playful, Creative. ____

B. Dedicated, Observant, Conscientious. ____

C. Compassionate, Sensitive, Warm. ____

D. Adaptable, Persuasive, Charming. ____

E. Imaginative, Reflective, Calm. ____

F. Responsible, Logical, Organized. ____

(Answers on Page 161)

Walter Workaholic,

Director of Operations,

reads the IMMEDIATE ATTENTION memo just delivered by courier from the CEO:

> **Corporate Headquarters requests a contingency plan for a 10 per cent budget reduction, all departments. Need a preliminary response from your department no later than noon Wednesday.**

"Mrs. Doherty, will you make three copies of this memo?" Walter asks his secretary. "And would you mind telling James, Michelle, and David to come to my office immediately?" Walter asks his key staff to read the memo. "As you can see, we need to put our heads together and generate a group consensus concerning the budget. And we don't have very much time. What options do you see?"

"Walter, in my opinion, we ought to...." Walter listens attentively to James, then interjects: "We don't have the luxury of opinions. We need recommendations based on solid factual foundations. Will each of you take the time this morning to think this through properly and gather the facts we need to support a workable budget cut? Can everyone meet again at 11:15?"

Ruby Reactor,

Director of Public Relations,

tells Cindy that her problems will gradually fade away "as long as you continue to work together with everyone else on the staff. You are an important member of our public relations team, Cindy. The better you feel about yourself, the better your work will be." With that compassionate advice, Ruby sends Cindy back to her copy writing and turns to the agenda her secretary has prepared for today.

The morning schedule includes a meeting with staff from another department, an interview with a reporter from New York, and a preview of the new slide and sound show for the marketing department. The afternoon is open except for the mysterious meeting of department heads.

"I really need to talk with Peter before we unveil the new slide show for his department," Ruby considers. *"I need to let him know how concerned all of us are about the people in marketing. That kind of intra-department harmony will go a long way toward helping this company grow."*

Paul Persister,

Director of Finance,

reads the memo requesting budget cut contingency plans, picks up the telephone, and rings his assistant director's desk. "John, could you stop what you're doing and come to my office? Good."

Paul hands John a copy of the memo. "John, what do you believe should be our most important considerations in responding to this memo?" he asks. "It is my opinion that any contingencies we devise could very well become realities, so we need to be as thorough and conservative as possible."

Paul listens respectfully to his assistant's evaluation of the memo and its portent. "Those are excellent ideas, as usual," he says when John concludes his initial recommendations. "Will you tell key staff to look carefully at the facts and be ready to give me their opinions of the situation later this morning? Then I can make the preliminary decisions according to the CEO's timetable."

Doris Dreamer,

Director of Environmental Services,

carefully scrutinizes the neat stack of job completion checklists submitted by Robert, the night supervisor. *"Robert is always so direct and clear....not like Albert,"* she ruminates. *"Things would go so much smoother if Albert would tone down some and pace himself."*

Doris contemplates the voluminous body of checklists, preventative maintenance calendars, and inspection reports. From this diverse stream of paperwork, she draws a complete and accurate daily picture of the corporate environment. A knock on the door breaks her concentration. "Come in," she says quietly. It's Rhonda, executive office housekeeper.

"Yes, Rhonda."

"Mr. Schwartz said we need to increase the watts in his lights," she says.

"OK," Doris replies, then looks away.

"But Mr. Schwartz said he needs more light right now," Rhonda urges.

"Doris, remember it is your job to be more explicit. Like it or not, you do have to provide direction."

Doris looks at Rhonda. "Go see Albert. He'll get the light bulbs for you."

Rita Rebel,

Director of Special Projects,

dashes into the foyer of her departmental offices with her usual flair and enthusiasm. "Look alive, oh ye burners of the midnight oil," she shouts to a group of employees. "And you, Zeke. Are you primed to exercise that dulcet voice of yours today? I've got a new telephone survey just waiting to be unleashed on our West Coast customers. How's about dropping by my desk when you get a chance later this morning."

"Late again, I know," Rita announces in mock apology to Penny, her indispensable administrative assistant/secretary. "Anything hot?" Penny hands her the CEO's memo on budget reduction contingency plans. "Wow!" Rita whistles. "This is a hot one. Let's call together the troops and see if anyone can figure out how to stave off the wolves. But first I've got to make a few calls."

Rita dials the marketing department. "Hey, Peter, have I told you lately how much I like working with you?" Rita says. "Now, about that memo...."

Peter Promoter,

Director of Marketing,

is concluding his conversation with Rita: "....and don't sit on this one, friend. The people upstairs mean business, so you had better move swiftly and decisively, if you know what I mean. Gotta go."

Peter calls his international sales manager into the office. "Alice, cancel your plans for this morning, take this memo, and find three areas in your operations that could stand a budget cut. Report back to me at 11. And tell Bart to come in."

"Bart, Rita in Special Projects tells me they're exploring the possibility of establishing a new computer tracking system to monitor the commissions of your road reps. You know as well as I do that our people have the flexibility to adjust their margins to close a deal. Tell me how we can structure this thing, bottom line."

Before Bart can step out the door, Peter is dialing the phone. *"Can't figure this 2 o'clock meeting. Maybe Schwartz has an inside line on what's going down...."*

Management styles....

One of the fastest ways of knowing what management style to use with each of your people is to observe how they interact with others.

People who frequently give commands, imperatives, or orders without attacking in their normal interactions and are action (task) oriented are letting you know they will do best when you use an **autocratic management style.**

People who frequently request information, or ask questions in their normal interactions, and who are task oriented, are letting you know they will do best when you use a **democratic management style.**

People who frequently are nurturing in their normal interactions, and who are more people than task oriented, are letting you know they will do best when you use a **benevolent management style.**

People who frequently are playful and joking in their normal interactions are letting you know they will do best when you use a **laissez faire management style.**

Applying what you have just read (observed) about our six characters, which management style is best to use with each Personality Type?

*P*ersonality *T*ype

1.	Reactor.	4.	Dreamer.
2.	Workaholic.	5.	Rebel.
3.	Persister.	6.	Promoter.

*M*anagement *(Interaction) S*tyles

A. **Autocratic** (Directing)   ____   ____
B. **Democratic** (Requesting) ____   ____
C. **Benevolent** (Nurturing)   ____
D. **Laissez Faire** (Playing)

(Answers on Page 161)

Walter Workaholic

glances at his memogenda, then at his contemporary desk clock, which is synchronized precisely with the grandfather clock in the CEO's office. (Mrs. Doherty checks monthly with the CEO's secretary to confirm the synchronization.) *"Fifteen minutes until my next appointment. Time enough to organize my thoughts on the reorganization plan for shipping and distribution."*

Nine minutes later, Walter caps his pen, lays it squarely in its place next to his personal computer, and pauses to study the symmetry of the framed awards and certificates on the opposite wall. *"That plaque from International Headquarters for Outstanding Achievement adds a real sense of order to the display,"* he thinks. *"But the production graph on the easel is crooked. Can't stand that."*

Walter straightens the graph, checks his wristwatch. *"Still five minutes until my appointment."* He steps outside his office to Thom Walker's desk. "Good work," Walter says, looking over his inventory manager's shoulder. "Your ability to synthesize data continually amazes me, Thom."

Ruby Reactor

likes to pamper her senses before plunging into the hard-nosed demands of doing business. To counter a slight feeling of uneasiness about the P.R. staff meeting she has called to discuss budget cuts, Ruby closes her office door, settles back into her comfortable chair, and soaks in the nourishing environment.

"They look so young and alive....how blessed I was to have them as parents," she reminisces. The yellowing photo of mom and dad occupies a prominent position on her desk (next to a photo of her brother, sister-in-law, and two nephews). Cozy furniture and soft, earth-tone colors blend nicely with the lush green of spiraling philodendrons and the inviting scent of potpourri. *"Surely there's a way I can approach this budget cut planning without threatening anyone...."* Ruby's secretary knocks quietly and says, "Staff meeting in two minutes."

"Thank you, Ellen," Ruby says. "I really appreciate how sensitive you've been to my concerns over this budget matter. I certainly feel a lot better having you there to support me."

Paul Persister

puts the departmental organization chart on his uncluttered desk and pauses to study the photograph of himself shaking hands with the governor. *"Now there's a man who knows how to put his convictions into action. Winning his respect and loyalty is one of the highlights of my life."* The photo stands discretely on a traditional mahogany credenza beside the latest addition to Paul's office decor -- an aquarium. *"I ought to take the time to learn the names of those exotic looking fish,"* Paul decides with a modicum of self-mockery. *"But Kathleen said their presence would help my high blood pressure, and I'm beginning to believe she's right."*

Paul checks his watch. *"Harkness' opinion is usually solid. I'll get his evaluation of the budget priorities."* Slightly off center because of the surprise morning memo and the mysterious afternoon meeting, Paul tarries for a moment at his antique étagére to straighten his valuable collection of porcelain birds.

At his senior auditor's desk, Paul says: "Harkness, I've always valued your judgment. Concerning our budget priorities, in your opinion should we...."

Doris Dreamer

is never one to get overly excited. The pulse of this day, however, seems to be coursing with unusual swiftness. *"First the mystery meeting, now the sharpening of a budget knife,"* Doris muses, turning her reflection outward. The CEO's budget memo motivates her to action. She, in turn, directs her secretary to page every department head and supervisor. Now, in the quiet isolation of her plainly furnished office, she listens calmly to a rapid series of phoned-in recommendations and suggestions from her staff.

"Give me a calm and steady beat....the many unified dynamos, the coherent motion of pistons," she reflects with her usual wry and private wit after hanging up from one such conversation. Doris looks away from her notes to the bookshelf: science/engineering periodicals, technical manuals, and the little section of poetry volumes -- the only adornment in an office otherwise bare of pretense, frills, or indulgences. The phone rings again. "Tell me, Edgar," Doris says. "Where can you trim the budget in your section?"

Rita Rebel

crumples a piece of paper and tosses it at the miniature basketball goal on top of the trash basket in her office. "Swish!" she chuckles. "Wish this budget business was so easy."

It's a rare day when Rita's office door is closed. Today is no exception. She tears off another piece of paper from the scratch pad and tosses it at Zeke, her research supervisor, who just happens to be walking by the open door. He ignores the missile, Rita mutters a mock insult, kicks back her roller-ball chair (a mod aqua-blue model with built-in stereo speakers hidden in the moulded headrest), and turns her gaze to the paired Andy Warhol prints in chrome frames on the opposite wall. *"Bet ole Andy didn't care a buffalo berry about budgets. Then again, he didn't have my innate business acumen. Guess I'd better call in my resident numbers crunchers and office Vulcans to help me deal with this budget mess."*

Impulsively, Rita leaps from her chair and dashes to the door. "Now hear this, now hear this," she shouts. "Anyone who wants to save their paycheck or reputation, report front and center...."

Peter Promoter

is moving through the morning with characteristic alacrity. He is dipping and darting through the sea of daily business like the mighty stuffed marlin so prominently displayed on the wall behind his massive teak writing desk with its hand-tooled leather top.

Perched confidently on the edge of his thick, high-backed, black leather chair, Peter fixes his focus on three immediate challenges: finding an inside angle on the afternoon meeting, covering his flanks on budget cuts, and nailing down plans for this weekend's junket to Vegas.

(Peter had thought nothing of paying two grand last weekend for a set of rare Flemish pewter flagons -- ostentatious bookends indeed! *"Expensive curios make distinctive status symbols,"* Peter surmised, *"and besides, they can be turned quickly back into cash if need be."*)

Peter dials his direct sales manager. "Markowitz, find out what's up for the two o'clock meeting, and your weekend starts on Wednesday."

Motivational strategy....

One of the best ways to know how to motivate your people is to observe how they compliment, praise, or motivate others. What they like in others often is what they themselves desire. How they arrange their desk or office also helps you discover a great deal about their motivational needs.

Based on your observations of our six characters in their office environment, as well as your appraisal of their motivational methods with subordinates, what is the motivational strategy best suited to each Personality Type?

Personality Type

1. Reactor.
2. Workaholic.
3. Persister.

4. Dreamer.
5. Rebel.
6. Promoter.

Motivational Strategy

A. Recognize hard work, dedication, values and commitment. _____

B. Accept the person without conditions. Spend time to make personal contact. Let them have a sensory filled, cozy work area. _____

C. Recognize hard work and be clear about time structures. Give awards, certificates, or plaques. _____

D. Give immediate rewards, bonuses, trips, perks, etc. _____

E. Be playful and encourage creativity--allow fun environment. _____

F. Be direct and let them have their private space. _____

(Answers on Page 161)

The
Plot

The Plot

The mystery
of the 2 p.m. meeting is
about to unravel, or perhaps it will
explode: We shall see. (These can
be much deeper waters than you
think.) We do know that the mind
reveals its nature through every
action and reaction, every gesture
and expression. As our characters
gather in the conference room
and the plot begins to thicken,
pay attention to their movements.
Whom they seek out in the crowd
(if anyone) will reveal their
Environmental Preferences,
which hold another key to
masterly management.
Then, after the conference
ends, observe how each
character reacts to the
startling news. Their
Perceptions are
additional clues to
Personality Type
and to their
view of the
world.

- **E**nvironmental
  Preferences
- **P**erceptions

At 1:45 p.m. sharp, **Walter Worka-holic** enters the executive conference room. The first department head to arrive for the 2 p.m. meeting, he notices the conspicuous absence of the usual assortment of beverages, which are standard fare for executive staff meetings. It's a small aberration, but one that sends up a red flag. *"Something is not in its right place,"* he thinks. Walter straightens his tie, tugs on his suit jacket, and walks over to a junior executive from marketing, who is the only other person in the room..

A minute or two later, **Doris Dreamer** and two of her staff enter the room as if they are on a special mission. Indeed, they are. One of the men holds a thermometer and humidity gauge, the other carries a ladder. Doris, disregarding the other people in the room, refers to a checklist and quietly directs the men, who are analyzing the quality and flow of air from vents near the ceiling.

The stylish cut of her dress, the pleasing blend of hue and sensibility in her make up and hair style, and the aura of harmony and confidence in her deportment -- a striking combination of femininity and professional bearing -- turn a head or two when **Ruby Reactor** enters the conference room. Two close associates are with her, and the three of them exchange brief civilities with others before joining an intimate little circle of like souls in one corner of the room. Despite her outward display of power, Ruby's inner voice hears a convoluted chorus of emotions. *"Walter looks deeply concerned....I hope he doesn't feel like our departments are in competition over these budget cuts."*

Paul Persister, his neatly pressed suit the epitome of conservative style, steps inside the conference room and pauses to observe the scene through intense, piercing eyes. He formulates a quick judgment: *"These people are wearing their game faces. Deadly serious. We're in for something profound, I believe."* He notices Walter. "If there's anyone here I can trust, it's he." Paul walks toward Walter, but **Peter Promoter** intercepts him. "Tell me, Paul, doesn't this suspense get your juices flowing? Let me in on the latest about what's coming down."

Peter realizes quickly that his associate in finance has no inside information to divulge, so he turns away to seek another source. He stops briefly to chat with a group from operations, then notices the senior vice president's administrative assistant entering the room. "Now there's the right man to see. I'd better get to him before anyone else does."

Five minutes to two, and the room is buzzing. Doris dismisses her staff, takes a seat between two empty chairs, and buries her nose in paperwork. Paul engages Walter in animated conversation. **Rita Rebel,** wearing an oversized button displaying "Day Care 'Cause We Care" in bold pink and blue letters, dashes into the room with a burst of energy. The button is intended to generate interest in her new project for worklife enrichment.

Rita stops at Ruby's circle just long enough to hand out buttons, then slips away to share a joke with the group from marketing. "Boys, I've got a good one,"

she says, but that's as far as she gets. All
eyes turn toward the distinguished gentleman entering the room. A hush falls.

That gentleman is the senior vice
president, known to everyone by the
weight of his initials. A cold chill per-
meates J. W.'s every word and gesture as
he announces matter-of-factly that the corporation has been acquired by an international conglomerate. "There is no reason
for concern at this time," J. W. says. "We
have been advised that this corporation
will be merged with Consolidated International, but that no personnel or operational
changes are anticipated. I have no further
information to divulge at present, and I
will not entertain questions. The meeting
is adjourned."

Environmental preferences ....

By observing how people consistently spend their time, especially when they are allowed to choose where they prefer to be, you will gain invaluable information about environmental preferences. This information will help you place people in their most productive environment.

You have seen the normal behavior of our six characters during the few minutes preceding the mystery meeting in the conference room. Based on your observations of where they moved and stood, see if you can match each Personality Type with their most effective environment.

Personality Type

1. Reactor.
2. Workaholic.
3. Persister.

4. Dreamer.
5. Rebel.
6. Promoter.

Environmental Preferences

A. One-To-One.   ____   ____

B. Group.   ____

C. Alone.   ____

D. Group-To-Group. ____   ____

(Answers on Page 161)

J. W., his staff trailing closely on his heels, closed the door to any questions from his department heads by immediately leaving the conference room.

An eerie silence of many seconds was followed first by nervous coughing, uneasy laughter, and several ahems, then by the quiet rumbling of uncertain conversations.

The primary concern, whether admitted or not, was job security. The question running through everyone's mind, in one form or another, was simple:

"What's going to happen to me?"

Ruby Reactor, sitting directly across the conference room table from Walter and Paul, sighed deeply and said: "I just can't turn my feelings off. I'm so uncomfortable not knowing what is going to happen to us. All of you have become family to...."

Walter Workaholic, the long furrows on his forehead deepening with the intensity of his thoughts, cut Ruby off before she could say the last word of her sentence.

"I think you may be jumping to conclusions about your job, Ruby," Walter said. "We don't know for a fact that we are in jeopardy of losing our jobs. We need to wait and get more information."

"I'm in agreement with Walter," **Paul Persister** said. The parallel fold between his piercing eyes seemed to cut sharply into his countenance. "I believe we need to trust in a company that consistently has been just and fair with us. It's my immediate opinion that all of our jobs are secure."

At the opposite end of the conference room, Peter rises to his feet, exhales forcefully, and turns to **Doris Dreamer.** "Doris, tell us what you're going to do."

Outwardly, J. W.'s bombshell announcement had not put even a small chink in Doris' stoic armour. Inwardly, a sudden image flashed through her mind's eye as Peter finished asking his question. *"The splendid isolation of an atom's innermost electron....Ordinarily, the world hardly affects it..."* But this was extraordinary. The familiar and the secure were beginning to spin on a new axis, not only for Doris, but for everyone who had listened to J. W.'s explosive message of change.

Turning to face Peter and looking calm and imperturbable, Doris replied: "I'm going to wait until somebody in authority tells me if they want me or not."

Peter **Promoter's** ruddy complexion took on a deeper shade of red as he turned away from Doris and said (to no one in particular): "Somebody has to go directly to the top and get the straight skinny."

Before his implied imperative could settle, Peter darted out the conference room door, uncertain about exactly where he was going, but driven by the urge to go somewhere, do something -- now!

Rita **Rebel** was doing a slow burn. Instead of emitting their usual twinkle, her deep blue eyes were flashing with indignation. She walked up to Walter and Paul and interjected: "I don't like this one bit. I want to know what's going on, and I want to know it now."

Perceptions....

One of the most important concepts to understand when you seek to motivate others is the awareness that each Personality Type views the world uniquely. By knowing how each of your people takes in information, you can be much more effective in motivating them.

Having just observed our characters give their views of the merger announcement, see if you can match the perception with the Personality Type.

Personality Type

1. Reactor.

2. Workaholic.

3. Persister.

4. Dreamer.

5. Rebel.

6. Promoter.

Perceptions

A. Actions.　　　　　　　　———

B. Emotions.　　　　　　　———

C. Reactions
   (Likes and Dislikes).　　———

D. Opinions.　　　　　　　———

E. Inactions.　　　　　　　———

F. Thoughts.　　　　　　　———

(Answers on Page 161)

The
Crime

The Crime

What is
going to happen to our
six uncertain executives? The
sudden turn of events, so
exceedingly provocative, has
led them from a secure and
positive management posture
to the brink of criminal
mismanagement behavior. In
this section you will observe
two degrees of mismanagement,
which are analogous to the
difference between a
misdemeanor and a felony.
What's more, the crimes
unfold in distinctive patterns
according to Personality
Type. Be alert to the clues of
language and conduct that
signal the emergence of
mismanagement behaviors
so you can detect and
deter similar crimes in
your sphere of influence.
Take a keen interest
in the details.
Of course!

- **F**irst **D**egree
  Mismanagement

- **S**econd **D**egree
  Mismanagement

Overly concerned about the feelings of her staff, **Ruby Reactor** walks into her departmental offices wearing a broad and cheerful smile. It masques her deeper feelings, which are churning in a whirlpool of emotion. Word of the announcement has preceded her arrival, thanks to the lightening fast corporate grapevine. Several of her people have clustered in a group to discuss it. Ruby gravitates toward them. *"Maybe there's something I can say to smooth over their fears...."*

"That old coot J. W. doesn't give a hoot about anyone," Ruby overhears as she joins the group. "Cindy, I know how concerned you are, and I really care how you feel about this, but J. W. was only doing his job," Ruby gently admonishes. "He told us there's nothing to worry about, and I feel sure everything will work out for the best." Unmoved, Cindy launches another verbal assault. Ruby, nodding her head yes when the manager in her says no, silently lets Cindy's behavior slide. *"I just don't feel like dealing with anyone's anger,"* she ruminates. *"Oh, dear, this can't be happening to us...."*

To display emotion, or indeed to show any outward expression of feelings in reaction to J. W.'s declaration, was simply not in **Walter Workaholics'** stylebook. He returned to Operations as if nothing had happened.

During the thoughtful walk between the conference room and Operations, however, Walter began to ponder the CEO's deadline for budget reduction recommendations. And now the deadline was burning hot in his pantheon of priorities. *"Getting our contingency plans precise and mistake free is crucial, and I can do that better, faster, and more efficiently than anyone else,"* Walter resolved as he stopped at Thom Walker's desk. "Do you have that budget analysis ready yet?" he asked. The inventory manager said he needed another half hour to finish it. "That's OK, I'll take it from here," Walter said, snatching the paperwork from Walker's desk and walking away without further comment.

"All I needed was just a little more time," Thom mentally responded. *"Just wait 'till the next time he needs my help on such short notice....."*

"When I set my sights on some-*thing, I hit it -- always,"* **Paul Persister** thought. *"I've had my sights on the top of this corporation since I came here, and I'm not going to let anything thwart those plans."* Paul responded to the acquisition announcement first by looking inward to summon his innate strength and courage, then by calling his staff together to assure them that everything will be fine as long as everyone keeps his head screwed on straight and follows his lead.

Now, poring over a complex statistical analysis of inventory depreciation schedules submitted by Harkness this morning, Paul notices a small transpositional error in one column of figures. He picks up the telephone. "Harkness, a second look at those depreciation schedules shows that one of the columns is out of order. I would expect a man with your experience to ferret out such errors before they reach my desk. We don't have room for error, now do we, Harkness?" Paul hangs up, notices the assistant director walk by his open office door. *"I wish he wouldn't wear such loud ties. No wonder he's still playing second fiddle at fifty five...."*

Uncertain about what to do next, **Doris Dreamer** walks in silence toward her office door. *"Where is the underlying unity...."* The urge to retreat into the strong cocoon of self is overwhelming. *"....in science, or in poetry?"* "I'm going to be in my office for the next couple of hours," she tells her secretary. "Please hold my calls." *"All I see is entropy, dissipation."*

"What about your 2:45 appointment with Albert?" Mrs. Sanchez asks. "He's completed that list of budget cut priorities you requested."

"I'm just going to put that on hold for now," Doris replies, closing the door behind her before Mrs. Sanchez can ask another question.

At her desk, Doris reaches half-heartedly for next month's blank preventive maintenance calendar. She scribbles a few lines, then puts it aside. She turns to a security document marked **CONFIDENTIAL.** *"Unusually heavy electrical usage in shipping and receiving. Humm. Do I really have the authority to deal with that?"*

At Special Projects, the staff knows it's best to keep a safe distance from **Rita Rebel** whenever stress creeps into the scenery. News of the acquisition announcement inspires everyone to be obviously and earnestly hard at work when their boss returns from the conference room.

This time, Rita is charged with her usual surface energy, but seems scattered mentally. *"I'm like a rat on a treadmill all of a sudden....can't seem to focus enough to get off dead center and get with it,"* she sighs.

Zeke approaches, asking Rita to clarify the data base universes for their West Coast telephone survey. "I just, ah, can't figure out what you're asking, Zeke old boy," she says, squenching up her face. "Why don't you check with, ah, check with Sammie on that one."

"Sammie, the Worklife Enrichment Consultant? Sure, Rita, she's a real data base pro," Zeke thinks as he leaves her office. And Rita? *"Whew. Sidestepped that one. When I'm like this, wish they'd make a few decisions for me...."*

An hour after dashing from the conference room to do something about the corporation's sudden, unexpected change of direction, **Peter Promoter** slips quietly into the Marketing Department offices. *"They're big boys and girls, anyway,"* he rationalizes. *"If my staff isn't capable of taking care of business by now, there's nothing I can do about it."* "Oh, Peter, there you are," his secretary exclaims. "The phone's been buzzing like a nest of hornets."

"Now, now Michelle. If you can't take the heat, you ought to get out of the kitchen," Peter replies as his customary charm dissipates. "Maybe so," she says. "Just the same, Rita in Special Projects has called three times." A subtle, parental tone edges into Peter's voice. "I don't have time to hold her hand on this one," he says. "I'll be in my office."

Bart, seeking direction on the computer tracking project, stops Peter at his office door. "Just handle it, Bart," Peter tells him. "But...." "No buts," Peter says. "You know the ground rules. Just do it." Peter turns away, leaving Bart standing there. *"I'm all for doing it on my own, but why won't he take time to give me all the information I need,"* Bart wonders.

First degree mismanagement....

There are six distinct mismanagement patterns. Their presence in a manager's behavior indicates that he or she has entered the shadowy realm of first degree distress. The first degree pattern also is a warning that the manager may be descending into another, more harmful mismanagement pattern.

Your awareness of these early signs of mismanagement gives you both the knowledge and the opportunity to intervene before major problems result.

See if you can match the first degree mismanagement behavior with each of the six Personality Types.

Personality Type

1. Reactor.
2. Workaholic.
3. Persister.

4. Dreamer.
5. Rebel.
6. Promoter.

First Degree Mismanagement

A. Passively avoids
making decisions.   _____

B. Finds what's wrong,
not what's right.   _____

C. Too concerned about
how everyone will feel.
Not assertive enough.   _____

D. Doesn't delegate well.   _____

E. Doesn't adequately
support people.   _____

F. Has trouble figuring
out what to do.   _____

(Answers on Page 161)

Feeling somewhat doubtful about her powers of discrimination, **Ruby Reactor** hangs up the telephone, ending a tortuous conversation with Paul, who had told her that he wasn't pleased with the slides she had selected for his Kiwanis Club talk. *"Why is he punishing me? Doesn't he like me anymore? I'm starting to feel as if I can't do anything right."*

Her features sagging with a droopy look of self-doubt, Ruby turns her attention away from the stack of transparencies and begins to search her desktop for the budget analysis file. *"I know I put that file somewhere. Ellen just gave it to me less than an hour ago. Where did I put it?"* Ruby wrings her hands. *"Just when I have to have everything running smoothly, I lose the most important file I've got...."* Ruby calls her secretary, who promptly delivers another copy of the file. "Ellen, you're always so efficient," Ruby says. *"And I'm getting so careless...."*

Alone in her office, Ruby tumbles deeper into an emotional dungeon of fear and rejection. *"Has J. W. ever really liked me?"* she broods. *"I just know they don't want me anymore. I'll get fired for sure."*

Caught in a swiftly moving stream of thought, **Walter Workaholic** tap, tap, taps his pen to a cadence of nervous impatience. Michelle stands uneasily at his desk. "The term budget implies operating with a fixed amount of money," he says. "Is that too much to expect from a so-called professional? Don't you ever just stop and think?" Walter dismisses Michelle with curt instructions to "rethink" the budget reduction priority list.

"These have got to be some of the most ridiculous attempts at logical reasoning ever formulated," Walter fumes, placing Michelle's list beside those compiled by James and David. *"I might as well make the budget decisions myself. My people just can't react quickly enough to make responsible recommendations."* Walter grabs a stack of papers from the In Box. They ignite his ire, rousing him to march out of his office. "Don't you ever check this work before routing it to me?" he barks at Mrs. Doherty. "A monkey types better at random than your clerks do on purpose." *"I ought to fire them all,"* he rages in a fiery furnace of thought. *"They can't even think for themselves."*

"**B**elieve me, John, there is only one way to formulate our response to the CEO's budget memo, and that's my way," **Paul Persister** tells his assistant director. "You had better tell that pack of whining numbers crunchers to quit complaining about long hours and do what they are told. I stay here until 6 p.m., night after night, and I expect your bookkeepers to give an equal commitment. Don't you dare blow this one, John. Those sharks upstairs are after us, and I'm going to have this department prepared when they start trying to chew on us."

A pensive glower settles onto Paul's features soon after John has hurried out of the office. *"I find it hard to go on believing in loyalty and trust and dedication in a situation like this one,"* he ponders. Paul glances at the Andrew Wyeth print hanging above his credenza. *"A stark field of wheat, the open window, bare bones simplicity. Is that all there is to beauty?"* Through his office door Paul notices a group of book-keepers. They are laughing, smiling. *"They sure don't have my commitment. If they're not with me, they're probably against me. I ought to fire every one of them before I get fired myself."*

"I'm not so sure I have the authority to decide that, Peter," **Doris Dreamer** told the caller. "I will do some checking and let you know tomorrow. Bye now." *"Fly me a parsec's distance away from the fray....I didn't bargain for all this pressure...."*

Doris buzzes Mrs. Sanchez. "Marietta, no more calls. None. *"I don't want to talk to those people out there...."* My head is really beginning to bother me. Another migraine I suspect. *"Let me ride unfettered on a steed beside the Green Night of the Midlands...."* Make a list of what absolutely has to be done before 5 o'clock. *"Wish they'd just leave me alone."* Bring it to me in a half hour. Bye now."

Doris glances at the Policy and Procedure Manual. *"I can find an answer to Peter's question in there. No need to consult anyone."* Searching through the index, she is sidetracked by a reference reminding her of astral projection. *"Or is it astrol projection? No matter. Sometimes I get so withdrawn it's like I can float above my body and look down on myself."* Mrs. Sanchez delivers the list. At the top in bold type is "Budget Reduction Priorities." *"Nobody has really told me what to do about that. I just know I'll get fired."*

Rita Rebel exhales with a loud huff of exasperation. "OK, OK. Give me a few minutes, will ya!? You didn't tell me you wanted it done that way. Listen, Peter, it's not my fault you don't know how to say what you mean." Rita hangs up before Peter can fire off a rebuttal. *"I'm so tired of always being hassled around here. If it weren't for all these goal-oriented, self-motivated robots, I'd be able to have some fun now and then."*

Rita, impulsive and fidgety, grabs a file and ambles to Penny's desk. "If it weren't for all the slackers and dead beats in this department, I'd have this budget priority thing done by now," she says, waving the file in the air like a traffic cop at rush hour. "And those big shot execs on the top floor -- they have it so easy, just sitting up there passing out directives while we sweat."

Penny, ever the optimist, offers a suggestion. "Yes, but that'll never work in the real world, woman," Rita snaps. The Wednesday noon deadline is bearing down on her like a freight train. *"Think they'll fire me, don't they. Ha! They can't do that to me. I'd show them."*

A devious little smile flashes across Peter Promoter's lips, then vanishes just as quickly when Alice enters his office. "Say, Alice, Bart just told me your international sales staff is loaded down with excess baggage. Suggested that your area of operations be cut 50 percent. But that's not why I called you in here. I want you to look at Bart's budget sheet and give me some feedback on his recommendations."

As Alice leaves, Peter buzzes Bart's desk. "Hey, Bart, you know the big boys are putting on the squeeze. Just thought I'd warn you that Alice is bad-mouthing your turf. She's been telling everybody your staff could do a whole lot more work with a lot less staff."

"The end justifies the means. Sure it does. Maybe a little in-house drama will shake them into action."
The phone rings. Randy, Peter's Vegas junket contact, reports that an early flight is available if Peter can break free. "No problem, pal. *"I can maneuver around these turkeys."* Besides, if they can't hold their own, who needs 'em. *"They'd better get outta my way."*

Second degree mismanagement....

When managers descend deeper and deeper into distress, each displays a distinct mismanagement pattern. It is a progressive pattern which manifests itself by degrees of negative behavior.

Knowing the behavioral clues to second degree mismanagement will help you retain valuable people, those key staff members who otherwise might (with or without a conscious awareness of their descent) sabotage themselves, others, or the organization.

See if you can match these second degree mismanagement behaviors with each of the six Personality Types.

Personality Type

1. Reactor.
2. Workaholic.
3. Persister.

4. Dreamer.
5. Rebel.
6. Promoter.

Second Degree Mismanagement

A. Makes mistakes. _____

B. Passively waits. _____

C. Manipulates. _____

D. Over-controls. _____

E. Pushes beliefs. _____

F. Blames. _____

(Answers on Page 161)

The Solution

The art
of detection leads invariably to
a solution. It demands that you
separate vital evidence from those
facts which are merely incidental,
and that you verify your solutions
in the crucible of reality. We can
state the solution to the mystery
of mismanagement succintly: it
is the mastery of management.
You become a master by *Assessing*
personality to determine the
specific *Psychological Needs* of
your peers and employees, then
by developing an individualized
Management Strategy to help
them satisfy their needs. You
have gathered many pertinent
facts during this investigation.
Now it is time to devise a
common thread upon which
these facts might all hang.
With this thread you
will weave masterful
solutions to any and
all crimes of
mismanagement.

- **P**sychological **N**eeds

- **A**ssessment

- **M**anagement **S**trategy

We've all heard someone say about another's behavior, "It's a mystery to me." Why do people do the things they do, especially the negative behaviors that cause disharmony, low productivity, and outright failure in situations and relationships? And what can you do to change negative behaviors into positives of harmony, high productivity, and across-the-board success?

Understanding negative behavior at the office (or at home for that matter) need not be a mystery to you. And knowing how to inspire your employees, peers, and family to leave their dungeon of negativity and move onto the level shore of positive action is simply a matter of masterly management.

One word encapsulates the mastery of management: **Motivate.**
And one concept holds the key to motivation: **Psychological needs.**

The six department heads in our tale of corporate America have descended into their private dungeons of mismanagement.

How can you help them turn back into the positive, productive people we met in the brilliant light of morning?

First, understand a basic fact of human nature--we are all motivated by our psychological needs. If these needs are not satisfied in positive, productive ways, then we will do negative, non-productive things in an attempt to fill these needs, often unaware of it.

A small child pulls on our coat, but we ignore him. Seeking satisfaction of his psychological need for recognition, he pinches us. If we scold the child, he has gotten our attention and satisfied his need, even if the satisfaction came through negative means.

Within each of us is a little boy or little girl with very real psychological needs. We will satisfy them--one way, or the other. By motivating others according to your awareness of their psychological needs, you will solve the mysteries of behavior and quickly become a master of management in your sphere of influence.

Reactors....

The Ruby Reactors of the world are motivated by being **recognized as a person** and by **sensory stimulation.** These two motivators satisfy a Reactor's basic psychological needs by recharging their psychic batteries and energizing the positive realms of their personality.

Reactors want to *feel* accepted. They want to be wanted. They want to hear their managers say, "I care about you," or "You're important to me." In the harmonious universe of the Reactor, coworkers are more than names and faces at the office. They are members of her extended family.

To motivate a Reactor successfully, you should move beyond self and relate directly to their psychological needs. Removing the blinders of self reveals a fresh vision of personality and lets you see the world through another's eyes.

A quick study of the relationship between Walter Workaholic and his Reactor secretary reveals what happens when a manager won't look beyond self-interest. Walter's world revolves around recognition of work. He assumes everyone else is motivated by work. After attending a seminar on the importance of praising the employee, Walter tells Mrs. Doherty, "Congratulations. You've increased your productivity by 20 per cent this month." Walter thinks he has done an outstanding job of motivation because he would like to hear that he has increased his productivity.

The result, however, is not what Walter intends. His Reactor secretary frowns, then says to herself, *"Why does he treat me like a number? Doesn't he like me? If he would just let me know that he wants me here, I'd work so hard for him."*

When her need to be **recognized as a person** isn't satisfied in a positive fashion, Mrs. Doherty begins to make mistakes. Although she is quite bright and very efficient, she is also a human being with basic needs. Making mistakes is her subconscious mechanism for getting negative recognition as a person.

When Walter points out her mistakes, Mrs. Doherty feels that he is attacking her. She might even say to herself, "Why is he punishing me? Doesn't he like me anymore?" She does not separate her behavior (her mistakes) from her identity (her person). When he criticizes her *behavior,* she feels he is criticizing her *as a person.* The fancy word is internalization. In everyday language, she is taking it too personally.

Why? Because she must get her need for unconditional recognition met -- if not positively, then negatively. Negative attention is better than none at all.

A Reactor's other psychological need is **sensory satisfaction.** Ruby Reactor and Mrs. Doherty need an environment that pampers their senses. Cozy, nurturing surroundings with flowers, plants, pictures of the family, candles, soft music, comfortable chairs, and pleasing colors meet the Reactor's sensory needs. A cold, stark environment will smother a Reactor's warmth and compassion.

A **Persister bank president deter-**mines that six employees who work in the foyer have too many flowers, plants, and pictures on their desks. He sends each the same memo: "Will you please remove all plants, flowers, and large (i.e., greater than 3 by 5 inches) pictures from your desks so that you may better see and communicate with our customers." In three months, one person quits, morale drops, and mistakes increase by an average of 12 per cent. The Personality Type of the six employees? You guessed it: Reactors, who need their sensory needs met as a significant motivator in their work.

As the bank president, what would you do?

A. Fire them all.

B. Replace them all with Workaholics and Persisters

C. Send another memo, letting them know they can have flowers, plants, and pictures in moderation.

D. Personally let them know they can have plants, flowers, and pictures in moderation.

ANSWER: .A na naht retteb si D a nehw emit eno si sihT

Workaholics....

The psychological needs to honor when motivating a Workaholic are **recognition for work** (praising his accomplishments) and **time structure** (establishing deadlines and schedules).

A Workaholic certainly knows when he has done a good job, but that knowledge in and of itself is not enough to satisfy his needs. Walter wants superiors and peers to confirm his work accomplishments by saying so. A voice inside cries out, "Praise me." The underlying basis of this fundamental need for recognition is the Workaholic's desire that people appreciate how clearly he thinks, and how hard he works.

"Walter, you did a great job," or, "What options do you see?" are solid, everyday interactional motivators to employ with a Workaholic.

Reward your Workaholic with plaques, awards, or certificates, which symbolize that people are aware of how hard and how well he has worked.

Negative recognition for work manifests itself on the job when the Workaholic doesn't delegate well and tries to over-control others. He justifies his behavior by rationalizing: "I can do it better, faster, and more efficiently." The result of his behavior is low morale, competition, and sabotage. Most of the time the Workaholic isn't even aware he is choking the company. Instead, he is convinced that he is right -- that he is the only one who can handle the job.

A Workaholic's descent into negative behavior has a profound impact on his personal life. His tendency to shoulder extra responsibilities, for example, leads to complaints of lower back pain. But the ultimate payoff comes when the distressed, negative recognition-of-work seeking Workaholic, who has devoted 14 hours a day, year after year, to his job, returns home to find the note:

"The children and I have left. I wanted a husband I could talk to, be with, and who would listen to my feelings. The children needed a father who would spend time with them and play with them."

And the **Workaholic's immediate** defensive reaction? "My god! Don't they know I did it all *for them!* " His entire life is based on the assumption that the world and all its inhabitants revolve around and respond to logic. If employees could just think clearly. If my wife would just understand that her feelings are something *she* can figure out. If my children can just learn to accept responsibility. He doesn't know that his Reactor wife must have unconditional recognition and his Rebel children must have playful contact.

He believes clear thinking will solve all problems. He survived and was successful that way. Indeed, his gift of superb logic serves him well in many areas of life. Yet, in distress he sees with tunnel vision, unaware that different Personality Types thrive on psychological foods other than logic and hard work. Hard work is important, but the idea that the best way to show love is to work now and enjoy family later may be nothing more than being right for the wrong reason at the expense of that heartbeat of life, the meaning of it all -- his family.

Time structure is the other psychological need of Workaholics. Be sure to let them know when projects are due. And remember, they plan their life in minute detail according to the clock, watch, and calender.

Negative time structure is expressed through the Workaholic's impatience and frustration when employees or peers are not on time, or when they fail to keep project time schedules.

On the home front, a Workaholic is likely to plan social events or a night at the movies according to tight, unrealistic, and self-obsessed timetables. He calculates the number of minutes it takes to drive to the theater, for instance, and devises schemes to avoid standing in line or having to stare at a blank screen. And if family members are not ready on time....well, woe be unto them!

Persisters....

The psychological needs that motivate Persisters are **recognition for work** and **recognition for conviction.** "I admire that about you....What do you believe we should do?....I value your opinion...." These comments ring sweetly in the ears of a Persister.

Like his close relative the Workaholic, Paul Persister needs recognition for his accomplishments at work. However, there is a significant difference between these similar Personality Types. A Workaholic concentrates on facts, and facts alone. A Persister seeks facts and opinions, attaching a value system to his quest for information.

Persisters usually have a great capacity to commit themselves to a task because of their belief in the value or importance of the final results. Like the Workaholic, the Persister listens to an inner voice that cries, "Praise me...." And the voice adds, "....not only for my accomplishments, but also for my commitments and beliefs."

You can help satisfy a Persister's need for recognition for conviction by asking for his opinion. To a Persister, being respected and admired is very important. Assign them to key committees where clear thinking and sound judgments need to prevail.

Letters of commendation, service awards, and everyday requests for their opinions are motivators that will appeal to a Persister's conviction needs.

At social functions, Persisters like to discuss politics, religion, or current events. Any of these conversational topics provide them with marvelous opportunities to express their opinions, beliefs, and convictions.

Negative conviction takes various forms in the Persister's work life. Some distressed Persisters push their beliefs with such force that people become annoyed or even non-productive around them. Other Persisters unyieldingly lock themselves into fixed positions on key issues "My opinion is the only right one," they decide.

As a result, they may become angry with peers who disagree with them, taking the attitude that "if they're not with me, they're certainly against me."

Crusading is another expression of negative conviction. A distressed Persister's crusade usually involves a very important mission or project he decides to champion. It is ironic that his passionate commitment and the forceful manner in which he expresses this commitment invites others not to hear him. He may become righteous, inflexible, prejudiced, suspicious, or bellicose in the midst of the crusade.

On the positive side, Persisters satisfy conviction needs in their personal life by volunteering for community service organizations, participating in local politics, or teaching Sunday School. They also achieve great satisfaction by role modeling their strong value systems to their children. Persisters take parenting very seriously and are dedicated to helping their children reach their highest potential.

In distress, the Persister parent might say to his son, who has just brought home a report card showing four A's and one B-plus: "What's the problem, son?" It won't be long before his son begins to wonder, "Why doesn't dad love me for myself? Am I only loveable when I'm perfect for him?"

Although this Persister is a loving and devoted father, his negative conviction behavior is counterproductive to his son's sense of security. Mr. Persister means well. He loves his boy and wants him to be the very best he can be so that his son can experience satisfaction, contentment, and the best of life. But in distress, he unconsciously invites misunderstanding.

When he needs even more negative conviction, the distressed Persister husband and parent will find what's wrong rather than what's right, and may preach at family members who don't subscribe to his enlightened opinions.

Dreamers....

Dreamers require **solitude** to satisfy their psychological needs and charge the dynamo that powers their personality strengths.

A Dreamer's need for solitude follows two streams. One flows inward, requiring alone time to run its course. The other flows outward into a secluded glade, requiring private space to reach its source.

If the language seems a bit imaginative, then it fits the profile of the Dreamer, who is introspective and reflective and calm. Dreamers also possess bright and original imaginations.

A desk or office off the beaten track provides some wanted relief. Dreamers do best when they are situated in a work space that insulates them from constant contact with others. Not that it's necessary to place your Dreamers in a hermitage. Just be aware that a Dreamer is most productive in a situation that doesn't require continual interaction with coworkers.

Management's best option for motivating a Dreamer to optimal performance is to provide specific and ample direction, then get out of the way and allow her to complete the job that has been placed before her. Within the secure framework of routine, a Dreamer will excel at tasks others would find tedious and mundane.

Giving your Dreamer a day off as a reward for a significant accomplishment will satisfy her need to break away from the din and the clamor so that she can recharge her batteries. A day off also will allow her to prepare for major projects and especially demanding tasks.

Dreamers are calm, easy going introverts who are solid employees. Just because they may not want to climb the corporate ladder doesn't mean they aren't company oriented. It simply means that a Dreamer's nature is not ideally suited to the demands of most management positions, chiefly because they lack the burning desire to expend energy interacting with others. The competent

Dreamer in a supervisory role would rather delegate wisely, shut the office door, and go to work.

Negative solitude surfaces in the workplace when a distressed Dreamer does not receive adequate direction or clear lines of authority from management. A Dreamer who falls into a negative behavior pattern will very likely withdraw deeply into self and appear not the least bit interested in her work.

Obviously, solitude by itself is insufficient to satisfy her psychological needs. The Dreamer also needs a clear and direct description of her duties and definite lines of authority to empower her to carry them out.

In their personal lives, Dreamers often live in rustic or secluded areas. They are accomplished in pursuits requiring great patience: making wooden cabinets, weaving, cultivating roses, or writing a book in the genre of Thoreau's *Walden Pond*.

D reamers need alone time to renew the psychic energy necessary for successful relationships. They get along well with significant others who can impart a firm sense of direction to the ebb and flow of the day, but who also have the good sense to ease out of the picture now and then to give their Dreamer companion room to breathe.

When a Dreamer is unable to find sustained intervals of privacy, distress intrudes and she may pull away from her loved ones because she lacks the energy to initiate meaningful contact.

A Dreamer parent in distress may ignore her children's accomplishments or their wishes even as she dutifully cares for their basic daily needs. She is present in body, but not totally present in mind or spirit. She loves her children deeply, but can't seem to mount the level of concentration necessary to pamper or entertain them. She also is likely to flit from one thing to another in an absent-minded state of passiveness. The only solution is an interval of quiet privacy and seclusion.

Rebels....

Playful contact is the primary psy-chological need for Rebels. They epito-mize the meaning behind the shopworn question, "Do you enjoy your job?" To a Rebel, enjoyment is essential to success in the workplace.

Contact to a Rebel means lively commu-nication -- the act of making a connection. You are connecting to a live wire, a high energy source of spontaneous enthusiasm.

The dynamic interplay between the closely related Workaholic-Persister Per-sonality Types and the Rebels of corporate America is particularly relevant to the mastery of management.

Some Workaholics and Persisters believe there is no place in business for people who refuse to subscribe to their fun-damental philosophy: *work now and play later.* Working now is the way these Per-sonality Types satisfy their psychological need for recognition for work.

Rebels, on the other hand, need to *play first and work later.* This fact of life does not imply that Rebels toy with their jobs. Play in this mature sense means upbeat verbal interplay, engaging banter, fun tasks -- any of the little daily amusements that one associates with a zestful, enthusiastic approach to life.

The manager who pays heed to a Rebel's need for such playful contact will open a doorway of unbounded potential. Rebels are the most creative of any Personality Type. They may not become the CEO, but they are likely to come up with the marketing strategies or inspired innovations that could save the company (and the CEO!).

Motivate your Rebels by joking with them. (Even a bad joke will do.) Show them you like to have fun with them. Assign Rebels to projects requiring a creative touch, then allow them to set their own pace. They will flourish without rigid time structure and close supervision.

A wise manager will make reasonable allowances for a Rebel's unique approach to interior decorating. Rita Rebel, for instance, would like her space to be filled with stimulating shapes, sounds, and colors. Posters and games, knickknacks and toys, lights and sounds -- these are some of her favorite things. And a desk or office in the midst of the din and the clamor is ideal for her.

Rebels in distress meet their negative contact needs through a variety of interesting outlets, none very playful. The energy a Rebel can devote to negative behavior often rivals the energy they generate in the positive mode.

Sabotaging a project certainly invites negative contact. Misfiling important papers often leads to a reprimand. Griping about upper management is a proven way to get attention. Selective hearing to repeated requests for a decision is a favorite ploy. And the reliable "Yes, but...." is always on the tip of a distressed Rebel's tongue.

In her personal life, the Rebel can satisfy her contact needs in the positive mode simply by having lots of fun. She gravitates to friends who are spontaneous, even a bit wild and wooly. Art and music stimulate her. Her home is busy with stimulation. She dresses for effect and attention, styles her hair to be different and unique. She plays hard because play energizes her to do the everyday nuts and bolts activities.

To get negative contact attention in her personal life, the distressed Rebel need look no further than her local Workaholic or Persister. If her Workaholic mate, for instance, lets her know that a clean, neat, and orderly house is important, all she has to do is be messy. She'll probably get her negative payoff. If her Persister parents have preached, "We keep our dirty linen in the house, so don't ever embarrass us in the community," then a guaranteed way for a Rebel to satisfy a negative contact need is to get drunk and go skinny dipping in the mall fountain just when the nearby city council meeting adjourns.

Promoters....

The psychological need for Promoters is **incidence**, the frequent occurrence of high intensity action. Promoters refuse to stand still and wait for something to happen. They need to make it happen, and now!

These are your high-risk players, consummate wheelers and dealers, the P. T. Barnums and James Bonds of the world. They seek to satisfy their incidence needs by orchestrating situations and events that will produce a great deal of excitement in a very short period of time. At his zenith, the Promoter becomes the principal player in the melodrama of his life. He longs not only to compete, but to win.

A Promoter's thick-skinned tolerance of the word "no" allows him to adapt to many situations that would stymie others. He is adept at persuading people to see and accept his point of view. He can turn on the charm with great power because seduction is his art form.

In business, Promoters are natural-born salespeople, excelling not only in direct sales, but also in marketing, recruitment, and fund raising. (You may have to devise the marketing plan, but the Promoter will make it work.) The act of selling becomes a direct extension of their personality. The product or service is secondary to the challenge of opening the door and closing the deal.

Promoters often play the role of entrepreneur. Their all-or-none philosophy and their tendency to move swiftly on a decision once it is made fit the demands of this risky business.

A manager can motivate a Promoter into positive action by offering quick rewards, whirlwind vacations, special one-time deals, and lucrative incentives *based on performance.* By attaching such perquisites to challenging, action-oriented projects, you will inspire your Promoter to top form. Just remember, he wants what he wants when he wants it, which is now!

Go right to the heart of the matter when you communicate with a Promoter. Talk about bottom-line expectations. The direct approach won't offend him. However, too many details, rigid 8-to-5 time structures, and long-term offers of reward will be counterproductive.

Provide your Promoter with healthy competition when you sense that he needs a shot in the arm. Timely motivational talks are also useful. By paying attention to him, you recognize his desire to stand out in the crowd.

In distress, Promoters meet their need for negative incidence by bending or breaking the rules to feed their hunger for excitement. Their justification is an "I'm special" attitude. Promoters also get their juices flowing by playing "let's you and him fight" games, in which they manipulate and maneuver colleagues into combative roles. Pitting one peer against another is their sure way to provoke excitement.

In power positions, Promoters incite negative incidence by making high-risk decisions that exceed their authority. With staff and employees, they may refuse to provide adequate support by expecting others to fend for themselves.

The personal life of a Promoter must be active and exciting to produce positive energy and self-satisfaction. Obviously, the opportunities to satisfy these needs are legion: flying lessons, Friday night poker parties, competitive athletics, SCUBA diving, white water rafting, quick return investments, plush homes, high performance sports cars, and expensive clothes and jewelry.

Negative incidence needs in a Promoter's personal affairs place him on the cold and naked edge of peril. He may gamble excessively, drive recklessly, or slip into amorous peccadillos -- all in search of the pulsating rush of excitement. A Promoter in distress may even manipulate close friends, leverage investments to extremes, or sell his soul for the thrill of the moment.

Assessment . . . .

Assessment is a necessary step in the process of creating of an individualistic management strategy. To motivate others according to your awareness of their basic psychological needs, you must first know their Personality Type. The checklists in this section will help you determine the Personality Type of co-workers. The checklists focus on basic indicators of personality: character strengths, personal appearance, vocabulary, environmental preferences, material interests, and distress behaviors. Match an individual to a Personality Type. Then you are ready to devise a motivational strategy for that employee.

Reactors

☐ Compassionate, sensitive, warm.

☐ Compliments and nurtures others.

☐ Well groomed (men); well-applied makeup (women).

☐ Meets people and makes friends easily.

☐ Uses feeling and emotion words.

☐ Fixes his/her desk/office to be cozy, comfortable: plants, pictures of loved ones, pleasant smells.

☐ Gets along well in a group setting.

☐ Under distress makes mistakes.

Workaholics

☐ Responsible, logical, organized.

☐ Likes facts. Asks questions.

☐ Articulate.

☐ "Worry" lines in forehead.

☐ Displays awards, certificates, or plaques.

☐ Goal oriented. Self starter.

☐ Over-qualifies and uses parenthetical expressions.

☐ Under distress over-controls and gets angry with people who don't think clearly or fast enough.

Persisters

☐ Dedicated, observant, conscientious.

☐ Often talks of politics, religion, or current events.

☐ Parallel vertical lines above nose.

☐ Values opinions; respect and admiration are important.

☐ Likes antiques or history.

☐ A solid company person with strong community or church ties.

☐ Invested in a quality, trustworthy, safe automobile -- BMW, Volvo, Mercedes, Saab, etc.

☐ Under distress becomes suspicious and crusades or preaches.

Dreamers

☐ Easy going, reflective, calm.

☐ Natural look, smooth face, even with age.

☐ Seldom starts conversations; usually a loner.

☐ Plain, stark office.

☐ Works better with things than people.

☐ Seldom shows any affection.

☐ Not competitive.

☐ Under distress passively waits for more direction (authorization).

Rebels

☐ Spontaneous, playful, creative.

☐ Artistic or musical.

☐ Easily bored; doesn't like 8-5 routines.

☐ Laugh and smile lines with age.

☐ Dresses for attention.

☐ Fun office: colorful, with posters or play toys.

☐ Lets you know what she likes and doesn't like.

☐ Under distress blames and is blameless.

Promoters

☐   Persuasive, adaptable, charming.

☐   Dresses expensively to impress.

☐   Bottom-line, action oriented.

☐   Uses autocratic style.

☐   High risk, lives for today.

☐   Quick reward oriented; commissions or bonuses.

☐   Uses jargon.

☐   Under distress manipulates.

Motivation . . . .

Motivation is the act of helping someone else satisfy their basic psychological needs. The goal of motivation is positive behavior: harmony and efficiency, maximum productivity, and bottom-line success. In the absence of positive motivation, people in business may descend into private basements of negative behavior. Then the workplace becomes a crime scene where flawed judgments, hurt feelings, and broken lines of communication lead to turnover, absenteeism, low morale, mistakes and injury, and employee sabotage.

Now that you know the system and the method for identifying the Personality Type of your key employees and coworkers, you can devise an individualized management strategy based on the psychological needs of your key people. When implemented with diligence, sensitivity, and self-confidence, this strategy of excellence will allow you to apply the masterly skills of motivational management to your professional relationships.

Reactors

Character strengths:
compassionate, sensitive, warm.

Strongest traits:
ability to nurture others
and be a harmonizer.

Favorite management style:
benevolent.

Perception:
emotions.

Environmental preference:
group.

Psychological needs:
recognition as a person,
and sensory appreciation.

Motivate your Reactor*
into more productive behavior by:

1) Saying,"I'm glad you're here. You're important to the company and to me."

2) Spending time talking about her family.

3) Publicly appreciating her.

4) Allowing personal touches at her desk or office.

5) Unconditionally supporting her.

Avoid:

1) Using an autocratic style with commands or imperatives.

2) Pointing out mistakes or her behavior.

3) Putting this person in a stark environment away from others.

* Pronouns of gender in this section are meant to be interchangeable.

Workaholics

Character strengths:
responsible, logical, organized.

Strongest trait:
ability to take in facts
and synthesize them.

Favorite management style:
democratic.

Environmental preference:
one-to-one.

Perception:
thoughts.

Psychological needs:
recognition for work
and time structure.

Motivate your Workaholic into more productive behavior by:

1) Saying, "Great idea," or "Good job."
2) Giving him an award, certificate, or plaque.
3) Giving him difficult problems to solve.
4) Letting him know project time structures.
5) Recognizing his hard work and continued commitment to being responsible.

Avoid:

1) Being too personal.
2) Confronting his actions.
3) Cancelling any projects without giving logical reasons why.

Persisters

Character strengths:
dedicated, observant, conscientious.

Strongest trait:
ability to persevere and hold fast
to   values and beliefs.

Favorite management style:
democratic.

Environmental preference:
one-to-one (alone).

Perception:
opinions.

Psychological needs:
recognition for work and convictions.

Motivate your Persister into more productive behavior by:

1) Saying, "I value your opinion, what do you think we should do about...."

2) Giving a letter of commendation or service award.

3) Recognizing his dedication.

4) Letting him know what you admire or respect about him.

5) Appointing him to an important decision making committee.

Avoid:

1) Using an autocratic management style.

2) Power plays with him.

3) Any redefinitions, even in small matters.

Dreamers

Character strengths:
imaginative, reflective, calm.

Strongest trait:
ability to stay at a routine task.

Favorite management style:
autocratic (use with).

Environmental preference:
alone.

Perception:
inactions.

Psychological need:
solitude.

Motivate your Dreamer into more productive behavior by:

1) Telling her exactly what is expected and leaving her alone to do it.
2) Giving her time off.
3) Providing her with private space.
4) Being as direct, comprehensive, and precise as possible.
5) Clearly defining and documenting her authority.

Avoid:

1) Using a benevolent or laissez faire management style.
2) Placing her with many people, or where the environment is full of stimulation.
3) Assigning new and different projects without adequate directions.

Rebels

Character strengths:
spontaneous, creative, playful.

Strongest traits:
ability to have fun, enjoy the present.

Favorite management style:
laissez faire.

Environmental preference:
group-to-group.

Perception:
reactions.

Psychological need:
contact.

Motivate your Rebel into more productive behavior by:

1) Joking and being playful.
2) Letting her have some personal latitude with dress codes and office decor.
3) Assigning her to creative tasks.
4) Doing something spontaneously with her.
5) Bringing her a cartoon once a week.

Avoid:

1) Restricting her to rigid time frames.
2) Giving advice, preaching at, or lecturing.
3) Assigning projects that require long-term planning and everyday monitoring.

Promoters

Character strengths:
persuasive, adaptable, charming.

Strongest trait:
ability to make things happen.

Favorite management style:
autocratic.

Environmental preference:
group-to-group.

Perception:
action.

Psychological need:
incidence.

Motivate your Promoter into more productive behavior by:

1) Telling him what the bottom line is, and letting him do his thing.

2) Giving him immediate rewards.

3) Providing some healthy competition.

4) Having expensive perquisites.

5) Presenting unlimited financial opportunities.

Avoid:

1) Being wishy-washy or non-confrontive.

2) Giving too many second chances.

3) Giving responsibility and accountability for long term, managerial projects.

Epilogue

And,
they lived
happily
ever
after?

Epilogue

J. W. opened the massive mahogany doors to the CEO's office suite. The tall, trim, dignified executive entered with his usual confident stride, but before the doors could swish quietly to a close, he would glance at the elegant grandfather clock in the foyer to confirm his promptness. *"Four fifteen. Precisely on time. Perhaps the chief has received some new information on the merger."*

Fifteen minutes later J. W. departed through the same elegant doorway. In his left hand he carried a bound brief, a few loose leaf directives, Consolidated International's annual report -- the typical stack of paper from a meeting with the CEO. In his right hand he held a hardback book. He glanced at the cover as the doors closed behind him. *"The Mastery of Management....Wonder why he wants me to preview this book tonight?"* Then J. W. chuckled softly to himself with a logical realization. *"Doesn't really matter why, now does it? I believe the old man has his usual solid reasoning behind the request. I'll read it after dinner."*

That night, with the memories of a stressful day lingering in his consciousness, J. W. read the book and made a decision. He based the decision on inside knowledge about the merger and a touch of introspection about his own management style. The CEO had informed him that all department heads would be retained, some promoted. *"Maybe I could have been a bit more positive in making the announcement this afternoon,"* J. W. thought, setting the book on his nightstand. "I'll put this information to the test and try it out tomorrow." That's exactly what J. W. did. And here is what happened....

"Ruby, I appreciate you finding a few minutes to visit with me this morning," J. W. says as he takes a seat in front of **Ruby Reactor's** desk. "You have a very inviting office. Nice picture of the family. Please say 'hi' to Bob."

Ruby's genuine smile and friendly countenance encourage J. W. to proceed along his planned course of action.

"**R**uby, I understand how con-cerned you must be about this merger. I want you to know how important you are to us, not only as a competent public rela-tions professional, but also as a unique human being who genuinely cares about people. You've helped me realize the value that high touch has in this bottom-line, corporate atmosphere of high technology."

On his way out, he turns back to her and says, "Ruby, I'm glad I'm getting to know you as a person. And I'm glad you're with us."

"Maybe we've got something here," J. W. con-siders. The image of his beaming Director of Public Relations glows brilliantly in his mind's eye as he walks into **Walter Worka-holic's** office. "Have you got a few min-utes?" J. W. asks. "I've got some facts about the direction of the company I'd like to share with our Director of Operations."

J. W. takes a seat and makes solid eye contact with Walter. "I read your cost savings plan for shipping and receiving late yesterday, and I must say that I'm thoroughly impressed with your ability to synthesize arcane reams of figures and formulas into solid solutions for the good of the company. I stopped by to let you know that your hard work and outstanding contributions have not gone unnoticed."

Walter's change in demeanor is obvious to the Senior Vice President. The other man's posture becomes more relaxed and the deep worry lines across his forehead fade away as J. W. continues. "Rest assured, Walter, that you will be on board and play a key role in this merger. There will be a major expansion and I'll be looking to you for input in the planning of critical path timetables for consolidation."

"That was really easy. I must have a lot of Workaholic in me," J. W. concludes en route to the next test of this bold new venture into the realm of psychological needs. *"Now Rita is a different story. She is going to be a challenge."*

Just outside the door of Special Projects, J. W. reaches into his coat pocket to make sure his secret weapon is readily available.

It is. He enters with as much of a flourish as he can muster. And there she is, standing with a small group of her staff. "Hey, Rita," he says with a smile (and a slight touch of nervousness). "Whatcha say we talk about an airplane ride." Out of his pocket comes a paper airplane, which he tosses above the startled group. "Sure, boss," **Rita Rebel** responds. "How about you and me sitting down in my office?"

"**R**ita, I'll just flat out admit to you, there have been times when I believed you played around too much," J. W. began. "And I thought that kind of behavior meant that you're irresponsible. But I'll tell you, I was totally wrong. I've come to realize that your playful attitude is a vital part of your creative energy." The senior executive leaned forward and smiled. "We be talking judge the book by the cover, but I'm reading you loud and clear now."

All Rita could mutter was an amazed, "Wow," but the twinkle in her eyes told J. W. all he needed to know. "Now about that paper airplane, Rita. It's your ticket on the corporate jet to L.A. Since you're going to play a big role in this new scene around here, I've landed a new project for you out in sunny California. We'll talk details tomorrow. See ya."

Rita simply couldn't contain her energy any longer. "Yeessss!" she peaks. "You got it, boss."

The gait in J. W.'s step is lively and confident as he heads for the next stop on this ascendant hegira. Now, approaching **Paul Persister's** office, he redirects his management strategy to match another Personality Type. This visit is special.

"Paul, I want you to know that you are a great source of strength to me, and I hope you don't mind if I call upon that strength in this time of change," J. W. said. The Senior Vice President looked upon Paul as a kindred soul, so his words flowed with ease and alacrity. "Your unwavering loyalty to this company and your deep sense of commitment to excellence have served you well. And me for that matter."

The Director of Finance listened to his mentor with a sense of awe and humility. Despite Paul's belief in the strength of J. W.'s commitment to their professional and personal friendship, Paul had harbored moments of doubt and outright fear since yesterday's announcement. Now, the genuine respect from the man sitting across from him had swept away all negativity in an instant.

"I'm really proud to tell you, Paul, that the CEO has selected you to be our next Vice President. You've earned it, not only for your dedication to your position, but also because you are such an admirable representative of this company in the community at large."

J. W. rises from his chair and shakes Paul's hand. It's a handshake of profound meaning, Socrates to Plato, a fraternal gesture of welcome into the upper echelon of corporate excellence.

Peter Promoter's office is just down the hall, but J. W.'s deep sense of pride in his protegee Paul is so much with him that pauses in the hallway in preparation for yet another challenge. It takes him but a moment to attune his thinking to another set of psychological needs.

"Peter, bottom line," J. W. announces matter-of-factly. "There's big change ahead with the merger, and everybody here is going to be on board but you." To the Director of Marketing, J. W.'s remark ignited a rush to equal all rushes. His eyes narrowed and his nostrils flared.

"No, Peter, you will be on board the Concord to Paris, where you're going to head up our new office for international sales. That's not too hard to take, is it?"

Flashing his familiar, confident smile, Peter replies, "I can handle it."

J. W. reaches into his breastpocket and pulls out an envelope marked *First Class*. "In the meantime, Peter, tickets to Vegas," he says. "Enjoy."

By now the chain of interpersonal successes that J. W. has engineered through astute application of this new-found management strategy lifts the experienced, worldly-wise senior executive into a buoyant, supremely confident frame of reference. *"Like a kid in a candy store,"* J. W. allows himself. *"I do believe the CEO has discovered something quite novel and most definitely valuable."* Then he remembers **Doris Dreamer,** the quiet one in her secluded room. *"Ah, the last of this morning's mysteries, and not an airy nothing, this one,"* he determines. *"The final problem...."*

Doris greets her immediate superior with concise professional courtesy. She closes the office door, invites J. W. to have a seat, slips lithely into her chair, places her hands in her lap, makes brief eye contact, then looks away as he begins to speak.

"Doris, I wonder if you've ever realized what a steady, calming affect you have on others? I'm beginning to see how valuable your unruffled nature is to the smooth flow of Environmental Services. And I've got to be frank with you. At times I've misinterpreted your reserve for a lack of involvement. I realize now that you weren't pulling away from your responsibilities, but simply energizing yourself for difficult tasks....tasks, I might add, that you handle with skill and imagination."

Doris no longer looks away. Instead, she gives J. W. her rapt, undivided attention. The unbroken eye contact between them tells J. W. that he has penetrated her panoply and opened a channel of positive communication between them.

"Now about this merger with Consolidated International," he continues. "You will be experiencing more authority, and I'll be expecting you to apply your imaginative abilities to solve any problems that arise. I'll be sending you detailed directives on your new responsibilites. And Doris, rest assured that you and your staff will have my total support and authorization."

J. W. stands up and offers his hand. "Thanks for staying with the company," he tells Doris. Her grip is firm, confident. "Why don't you take a few days off for a well-deserved break," he adds. "In fact, go ahead and take off tomorrow and Friday so you can have a long weekend. I'll see you Monday."

"Ha! It works!" J. W.'s reflections on his masterly morning of adventure and accomplishment reverberate through his consciousness with an electric enthusiasm as he enters the elevator and opens his book to the encapsulated descriptions of each Personality Type. The crease between his eyes deepens as he concludes, *"I believe I must be a Persister. Motivating people to reach their highest potential and truly support this company is a challenge I relish. I wonder if the CEO gave me the book for my people, or for me...."*

In an instant, it seemed, the gleaming brass doors were swishing open. There stood Mr. Semloh, the CEO.

"Good day, chief," J. W. said as he pointed to the book in his right hand. "I'm just amazed this works so well, yet seems so simple."

Mr. Semloh nodded. His smile was wry and knowing when he made his reply, "Elementary, my dear Watson."

The End

A Postscript

Did you identify your Personality Type? If your inward looking eye also happened to notice that certain traits, preferences, and behaviors from each Personality Type fit you, don't precipitate an identity crisis. What you saw about yourself is absolutely correct.

Though one Personality Type dominates your identity, each of the six types occupies a space in your mental, emotional, and social structure. The spaces that house each type are not equally furnished, however, and some are more accessible than others.

Either at birth or early in life, one of these types becomes your primary, or base, personality. You will retain this primary Personality Type for the rest of your life. But wait. Then, between the ages of one and six, the order of the other five types is established as your personality structure.

Think of your personality as if it were a six-story condominium. Your primary Personality Type occupies the first floor. At a given moment, you can enter your elevator, stop on any floor, and show the behavior characteristics of that Personality Type. However, you will have varying amounts of energy available to you on each floor. That is why most Persisters, for example, may move with ease into the floor housing their Workaholic, but have difficulty staying in their sparsely furnished Dreamer floor for very long.

Sometimes a person moves up to the next floor and "lives" there. During this time (usually from two years to a lifetime), he experiences the world as if he were that base Personality Type. Taking up residence on a new floor is called phase. This person is now motivated by the psychological needs of this phase (Personality Type). His entire life, both personal and professional, changes to reflect the Personality Type of his phase.

Phasal changes usually occur as the result of frequent and intense second degree distress. But regardless of phase, a person can step into his elevator and revisit any floor beneath his phasal apartment as long as his psychological needs are met positively. By making such a visit, the person reactivates all of the traits characteristic of that Personality Type. Such moves from floor-to-floor explain how a Workaholic (or any other type) can energize the Rebel, for instance, in his or her personality. However, his primary motivation will revolve around the psychological needs of his phase. Also, under normal distress he will show the negative behaviors of that phase.

The Mastery of Management will enable you as a manager to determine another person's basic psychological needs by identifying the Personality Type of his phase. Although a person shows positive attributes from many Personality Types, he will show the negative behavior of his phase. Most crimes of mismanagement are misdeeds of phase.

It is ironic that your knowledge of negative behavior holds the key to restoring your people to positive behavior. Yet, the crimes that a coworker commits (usually without an awareness of his wrongdoing) provide you with the necessary clues to identify his phase. And once you identify the personality phase, you can unravel the mystery of mismanagement by applying the techniques of masterly management to help satisfy a distressed employee's basic psychological needs.

Answers to quizzes

Character strengths.... (Page 47)

A	5	C	1	E	4
B	3	D	6	F	2

Management styles.... (Page 55)

A	4 6	C	1
B	2 3	D	5

Motivational strategy.... (Page 63)

A	3	C	2	E	5
B	1	D	6	F	4

Environmental preferences.... (Page 71)

A	2 3	C	4
B	1	D	5 6

Perceptions.... (Page 77)

A	6	C	5	E	4
B	1	D	3	F	2

First degree mismanagement.... (Page 87)

A	4	C	1	E	6
B	3	D	2	F	5

Second degree mismanagement.... (Page 95)

A	1	C	6	E	3
B	4	D	2	F	5

Authorized Websites/Email & Specialty Areas

For further information on the life and works of Dr. Taibi Kahler, Ph.D., as well as articles, books, endorsements, presentations, research on the Process Communicastion Model® and institutes of higher learning that have used the model, and for information on the clinical application, the Process Therapy Model©, you may contact Kahler Communications, Inc. or Taibi Kahler Associates, Inc. at www.taibikahlerassociates.com.
Email: kahlercom@aristotle.net.

In the U.S.:
Boys & Girls Clubs of America
   KahlerAtlanta@aol.com
Educational application
   www.kahlercom.com   joe@kahlercom.com
Selection, placement and career counseling
   RSMaris@aol.com
Spiritual/religious applications
   RSMaris@aol.com

Outside of the U.S.:
Delta Consulting
   www.deltacinfo@deltac.com
KC Austria
   www.kahler-communication.de
Kahler Communication Europe
   www.kahler-pcm.com
Kahler Communiciation Finland
   www.invoke-pcm.com
Kahler Communication France
   www.kcf.fr
Kahler Communication Japan
   www.kahlerjapan.com
KC Germany
   www.kahler-communication.de
KC Switzerland
   www.kahler-communication.de
PSDCI
   www.johnparr@rosile.ro